Pruning Terminology: Buds and Bud Growth

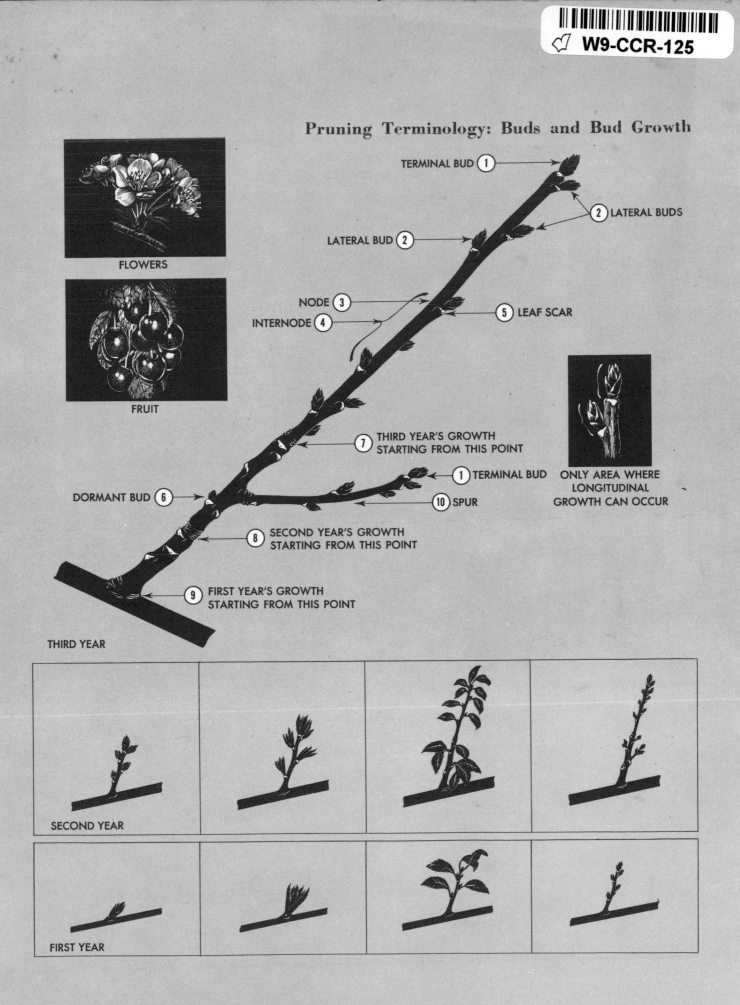

FLOWERS

FRUIT

TERMINAL BUD ①

② LATERAL BUDS

LATERAL BUD ②

NODE ③

INTERNODE ④

⑤ LEAF SCAR

ONLY AREA WHERE LONGITUDINAL GROWTH CAN OCCUR

⑦ THIRD YEAR'S GROWTH STARTING FROM THIS POINT

① TERMINAL BUD

DORMANT BUD ⑥

⑩ SPUR

⑧ SECOND YEAR'S GROWTH STARTING FROM THIS POINT

⑨ FIRST YEAR'S GROWTH STARTING FROM THIS POINT

THIRD YEAR

SECOND YEAR

FIRST YEAR

The
pruning
handbook

Roy L. Hudson

PAST PRESIDENT, CALIFORNIA HORTICULTURAL SOCIETY

DIRECTOR OF STRYBING ARBORETUM, RETIRED
RECREATION AND PARK DEPARTMENT, SAN FRANCISCO

Illustrated by Robert Blanchard

Galahad Books • New York

The Pruning Handbook by Roy L. Hudson
Formerly *Sunset Pruning Handbook* published by Lane Magazine & Book Company

Copyright © 1972 by Roy L. Hudson
Copyright © 1952 by Lane Magazine & Book Co.

Printed in the United States of America
Library of Congress Catalog Card Number: 73-92804
ISBN 0-88365-190-4

This edition published by arrangement
with Prentice Hall, Inc.

Contents

About This Book

Because pruning methods are founded upon natural laws of plant behavior, they are of universal application. A hardy shrub in Maine will respond to the stimulus of pruning in almost exactly the same way as a tender shrub will respond in Southern California or Florida. The difference is one of degree and timing. The hardy shrub growing in a rigorous climate, which enforces early dormancy and a long winter rest, will never make the amount of growth that the tender shrub will, in a salubrious climate with 365 growing days a year. The hardy plant may be pruned in fall, while the tender one should be pruned in spring. The hardy plant will require very little pruning, while the tender one may well lose up to nine-tenths of its framework. Yet basically the process is the same.

This book will attempt to explain the "why" and the "how" in the nontechnical terms of the amateur gardener. The timing will depend upon your location. A few miles latitude or a few hundred feet elevation will make a considerable difference in the optimum time for some of the operations described herein, so that location and the plant's condition rather than the calendar should be your guide.

Pruning, alone, cannot compensate for cultural mistakes. A plant's well-being depends upon many factors which cannot be discussed in a book devoted to pruning. In this manual it is assumed that your plant material is growing normally and that conditions of placement, moisture, pest control, and plant nutrients are correctly provided.

There is ample evidence that a general work on pruning has been needed. Many fine articles have been published, but few attempts have been made to gather a comprehensive survey of the subject into one volume. That the present effort will be carried into your gardens and help solve some of your problems and increase your pleasure in your trees and shrubs, is the sincere wish of the author.

ROY L. HUDSON

CHAPTER 1. Objectives of Pruning

One way to learn the fundamentals of pruning is to study the mistakes that other gardeners make.

You are doubtless familiar with the gardener who, at the first leaf fall, attacks his garden with saw, shears, and knife and cuts back everything in sight in one gigantic clean-up. Then, when each plant is stripped, he puts away his tools for the next year.

You may also have encountered his opposite, a sentimental soul who is fearful to cut into his plants beyond a snip here and there. Such God-given beauty, he reasons, should not be touched by human hands.

Somewhere in between comes the fellow who prunes all of his plants with a single tool, and the wrong one at that — the hedge shears. He painstakingly barbers his shrubs into domes, cones, and spheres, ignoring the natural forms of the plants.

Now, each of these gardeners betrays his own variety of ignorance of why pruning is needed in a garden.

The annual pruner overlooks the fact that different plants require pruning at different seasons. Not all plants are pruned in the fall. Some are cut back early in the spring, some right after flowering. Some are pinched back in summer. Thus, the grand sweepstakes pruning can very likely damage some plants by cutting them at a time when they are least able to withstand it.

The hedge-shears addict does more than offend the sensibilities of his neighbors by shaping everything alike. He actually interferes with the growth pattern of his plant materials. A few varieties thrive under this treatment, but most plants react with a prolific show of leaves and a snaggle of tiny branches that shade out and kill off the lower branches.

As for the timid gardener who fears to attack Nature's perfect handiwork, his hands-off policy can do more harm to his garden than his pruning shears. He overlooks the fact that pruning goes on constantly in Nature, for, as branches and leaves compete against each other for light and air, the weaker ones perish to the betterment of those remaining. This process, however, is untidy and slow. The same ends can be realized in neater and swifter fashion by pruning.

Thus it is that when the informed gardener takes his pruning kit into the garden, he may be planning to realize any one of several likely objectives.

Objectives of Pruning

General objectives of pruning have to do with modifying the growth of the plant to adjust it to the conditions of the garden.

The best pruning practice is that which accomplishes the desired end without destroying — or even over-encouraging — the natural growth pattern of the plant. At least the pruning practice should not mask or pervert the natural pattern of the subject in such manner that it becomes an ugly, characterless growth.

Some plants may require very little pruning to achieve these ends, depending on the plant and its place in the garden. Others may need a great deal of pruning.

Here is a run-down on the principal objectives of pruning in the home garden:

Maintenance of Plant Health. The first chore in pruning is to cut out all dead, diseased, or injured wood. This may be called the fundamental in all pruning. Diseased or injured wood is likely to spread infection to the healthy growth of the plant. In addition, all crossing branches should be removed to prevent rubbing, to allow more light and air to penetrate, and to prevent confusion of line in the structure of the plant. Thinning of weak, worn-out, or crowded stems is also important for the same reasons, and will improve the health of the plant, the quality of the foliage, and often the abundance of bloom. All of this type of pruning permits a more effective and

George Krebs, Photo

Health of a tree or shrub can be influenced by pruning. Here, branch at left forms weak crotch, likely to split from tree and damage it. Removal of branch will aid tree

complete spray coverage with considerably less effort on the part of the gardener.

Control of Growth. Shrubs and trees often outgrow their positions or become unshapely unless restrained by pruning. While perhaps not so important in some areas, the matter of pruning to size is of the utmost importance to the greater part of California where growth is very rapid and there is rarely a shortage of flowering wood.

With some varieties, pruning is needed to encourage the development of a natural form, particularly if the plant is growing out of its natural habitat. Ecologists tell us that it requires thousands of years for a tree or shrub to extend its natural range a few miles. Yet, we as gardeners attempt to grow plants from other countries and other hemispheres under conditions that may be directly opposite in every way, even to the complete reversal of seasons. The transitional period is only the time it takes a fast airliner to bring seed or scion to us. In a single garden may be found a tree from the Australian deserts, the Burma rain forests, our own Rocky Mountains, the hills of Greece, the high rocky plateaus of China. Instead of the natural conditions favored by each of these and the protection afforded by their close association in forest stands, they are usually planted as specimens in splendid isolation and given uniform conditions and care. Small wonder that the majestic tree described as a 200-foot timber tree in its native home is a dumpy, many-branched overgrown shrub during our own lifetime. This is especially true of plants moved from a warm and moist climate to a cold, dry garden. With judicious pruning, these imports can be encouraged to grow more closely to their natural form in a strange land.

Encouragement of Yield. Because of the blooming and fruiting habits of many shrubs and trees, maximum displays of blooms or bountiful crops of fruit can only be obtained by pruning. Plants that would naturally tend to produce a rash of small blooms can be encouraged to produce a smaller number of large flowers. Some that tend to grow their flowers and fruit in their topmost branches can be trained to bear them within reach of the average-sized gardener.

The yield of a garden shrub or tree does not always have to be fruit or flowers. Sometimes it is foliage. Pruning can be directed toward increasing the yield of leaves, where dense growth is needed for shade or where leaf color is interesting; or pruning can be used to shape the tree to direct the shade where it will do the most good. Thus, a spire-shaped tree can be pruned to umbrella-like form to cast shade in your own, rather than the neighbor's, garden.

Special Purposes. In many situations, pruning is used to train plant growth to fit special conditions in a particular garden. The natural form of the plant may actually be distorted to make it suitable for hedge, espalier, or dwarf specimen.

R. L. Hudson, Photo

Pruning can keep a plant within scale. This eucalyptus normally grows to great height. Severe heading and thinning each year keeps it small enough for street use

R. L. Hudson, Photo

How NOT to prune. Shrub corner with seven different species, robbed of natural beauty and individuality by "hedge-shears addict." Few shrubs thrive under shears

CHAPTER 2. Effects of Pruning

The basic principles of pruning are easy to grasp — once you understand a few simple facts about the way plants grow.

Let us take apart a typical woody plant and find out what makes it develop, and then apply this information to the techniques of pruning.

Plant Parts Involved

The typical shrub or tree has four main parts: a root system, trunk and branch framework, leaves, and seed-producing flowers.

Roots. A plant's root system may be composed of compact masses of threadlike rootlets or a far-reaching system of large, woody roots. Regardless of size, shape, or extent, all root systems serve the same purposes. They hold the plant in position and resist the stresses of wind and gravity. From the surrounding soil, they absorb water, which contains the nutrients needed for plant growth. And they serve as a storage reservoir for food that is not immediately needed by the plant.

Framework. All plants—whether they be half-inch alpines or forest giants—have a stem structure. The stem framework consists, in most varieties, of a central trunk with branches and sub-branches that all together make a pattern not unlike a well-developed root system.

The branches serve several functions. They hold the plant erect, of course, and they perform as a plumbing system to carry food and nutrients between leaves and

roots. The up traffic utilizes the inner core of the stem, the downward flow percolates through an outside layer which lies close to the bark.

Like the framework for a house — with its "studs," "plates," "rafters," etc.—the framework for a shrub or tree contains members that are identified by certain names. Since these terms are used frequently in this book, and in all literature about pruning, it is well to familiarize yourself with them. Those you will encounter most frequently are: the *leader,* which is a dominant branch that points skyward, usually a continuation of the trunk; *scaffold branches,* which are the main side branches; *laterals,* which branch off scaffold branches; and *spurs,* short branchlets that carry leaves, flowers, or fruit. These and other terms are illustrated in the drawing on the opposite page, which is repeated on the inside of the front cover for quick reference.

Leaves. Attached to the branches are the leaves — those incredible mechanisms that perform one of the miracles of the universe: the process of manufacturing food for the plant.

To put it simply, the leaf uses the energy of the sun to combine carbon dioxide, drawn from the air, with water and nutrients, drawn from the soil, to produce sugars and starches that sustain the plant.

Because the leaves depend upon the roots to supply part of the raw material used in manufacturing food, the root and leaf systems are nicely balanced against each

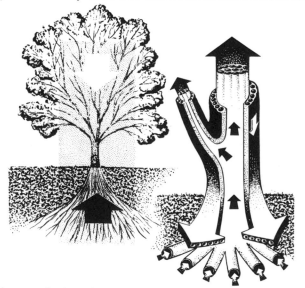

Water and minerals move up from roots to leaves through core; manufactured food from leaves comes down in bark

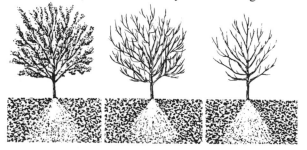

Pruning changes root-leaf balance. Branch-stored food reduced, but that in roots is funneled into smaller top

other. If the roots are reduced in volume, the foliage becomes less abundant; and if the foliage is greatly reduced, the roots stop growing and store less food.

Flowers and Fruit. Also attached to the branches are the flowers, whose sole mission is to create seed so the plant can perpetuate its species. If properly pollinated, the blooms turn to seed. The seed may be a mere speck,

Pruning Terminology: Plant Framework

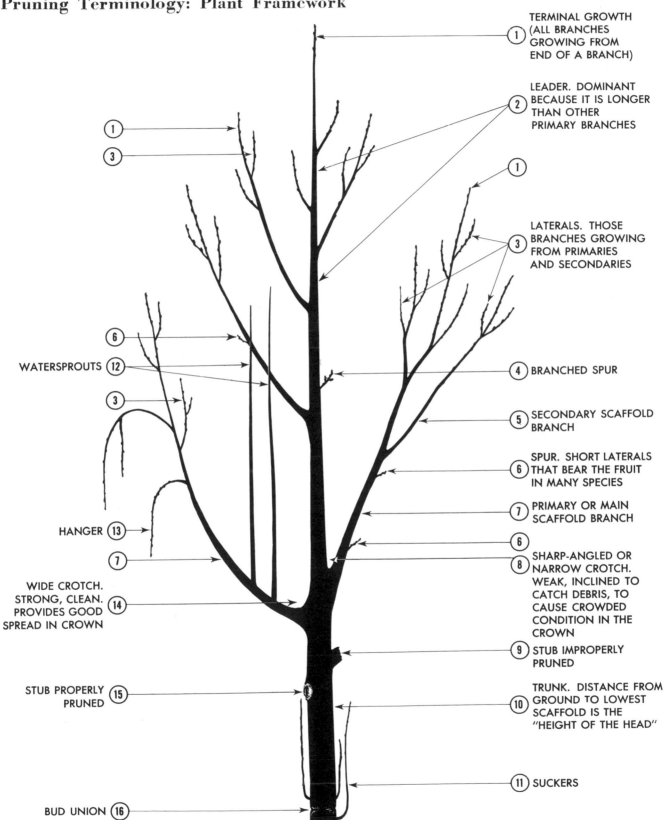

1 TERMINAL GROWTH (ALL BRANCHES GROWING FROM END OF A BRANCH)

2 LEADER. DOMINANT BECAUSE IT IS LONGER THAN OTHER PRIMARY BRANCHES

3 LATERALS. THOSE BRANCHES GROWING FROM PRIMARIES AND SECONDARIES

4 BRANCHED SPUR

5 SECONDARY SCAFFOLD BRANCH

6 SPUR. SHORT LATERALS THAT BEAR THE FRUIT IN MANY SPECIES

7 PRIMARY OR MAIN SCAFFOLD BRANCH

8 SHARP-ANGLED OR NARROW CROTCH. WEAK, INCLINED TO CATCH DEBRIS, TO CAUSE CROWDED CONDITION IN THE CROWN

9 STUB IMPROPERLY PRUNED

10 TRUNK. DISTANCE FROM GROUND TO LOWEST SCAFFOLD IS THE "HEIGHT OF THE HEAD"

11 SUCKERS

WATERSPROUTS 12

HANGER 13

WIDE CROTCH. STRONG, CLEAN. PROVIDES GOOD SPREAD IN CROWN 14

STUB PROPERLY PRUNED 15

BUD UNION 16

no larger than a grain of talcum powder, or it may be a peach pit, or a segment of a pine cone.

Plant Growth Cycle

Now, each of these major parts of the plant functions with varying degrees of efficiency and intensity, depending on the season of the year. Each plant passes through a yearly cycle that puts roots, stems, leaves, and flowers to work in different ways.

At some time during the year, usually early spring, a flush of life comes to most plants. Stored food, put away in the roots and branches the previous year, starts the plant on its growing season. The roots begin to push out, buds to open, and new branches, leaves, and flowers to form. The plant is off on its annual task of producing seeds.

If the plant is deciduous, it grows an entire new crop of leaves; if an evergreen, it puts out a new crop in addition to those already existing on the branches. The output of leaves is modest at first. The initial crop comes from buds formed the previous year. The new leaves go right to work to produce food while the summer sun shines. For several weeks, the plant continues to live on its stored food, but presently this supply is supplemented by that manufactured by the leaves.

Just before the seeds are set or the fruit ripens, most plants start their stem growth. New branches form and strive to make the plant follow its inherent shape, as far as it can under artificial conditions in the garden, where soil, shade, climate, paving, buildings, and other conditions often thwart the plant from reaching its ultimate size or natural shape.

When the seeds have formed, the plant's work for the year is done. All visible growth slows to a stop. No more leaves, flowers, or fruits appear, and the plant begins storing food for the following year. Food is cached away in roots and branches, and by the time cold weather arrives, the supply of next year's food is complete. The deciduous plant signals the finish of its active year by dropping its leaves; the evergreen goes dormant. The plant enters a state of suspended animation for the winter. When the soil warms up in spring, it starts off once more on its cycle.

This, in a capsule, is the history of a plant's year. Let us examine more closely certain stages of this cycle, because of their importance in pruning.

Bud Growth

A bud is simply an undeveloped branch, tightly packed and protected by bud scales, waiting for the proper stimulus to start lengthening out and developing. A branch can grow longer and a plant can grow taller *only* in or near the tip of the bud that is elongating during the plant's cycle of growth. When this elongation stops at the end of the growing period, another bud is formed for the following season. The bud from which branches develop is called a *tip* or *terminal* bud.

As the new branches develop, leaves are borne at intervals along the branch. These grow from *lateral* or *axillary* buds. They may be either opposite or alternate in their relation to each other. The point at which the leaf joins the stem is called the *node* and the distance on the stem between leaves is called the *internode*. The large majority of plants produce buds at the node, usually in the angle formed by the branch and the leaf called the leaf *axil*.

The lateral buds may or may not start into growth at the same time as the terminal ones. If they do not break at the normal time they are called *dormant* buds, and if they remain dormant for more than one season they are called *latent* buds. These latent buds are sometimes confused with the *adventitious* buds, which are far less common but are sometimes found. The latter are essentially buds that form, seemingly without reason, between the nodes on a stem, on the roots of some species, and even on the leaves of a few plants. Adventitious and latent buds rarely start into growth without some shock stimulus, such as the removal of a limb, but they can be very useful to the horticulturist who can initiate their development by pruning.

In many species of shrubs and trees the latent buds are capable of development for many years. They seem to elongate as the tree increases in diameter, though always connected to the annual ring in which they were formed. The bark usually buries these buds in time until their presence is impossible to determine by casual observation.

Bud Differentiation

All of the above types of buds are thought to be purely vegetative as they begin to take form. That is, they contain only the embryonic stem and rudimentary leaves. Somewhere in their development, if all contributing factors are right, a change takes place in some of these buds and they begin to develop flowers. This is known as *flower-bud initiation* or *bud differentiation*. The rest of them continue to develop as leaf buds. The time at which this change takes place is extremely variable in different species of plants. It is controlled in part by climatic conditions, but the deciding factor is one of food storage. When vegetative growth slows down in a particular plant, due to its reaching maturity or because it has used up most of the available nitrogen, the carbohydrates are no longer needed for foliage, stem, and root development. These plant foods then become available for flower and fruit formation.

Pruning Terminology: Buds and Bud Growth

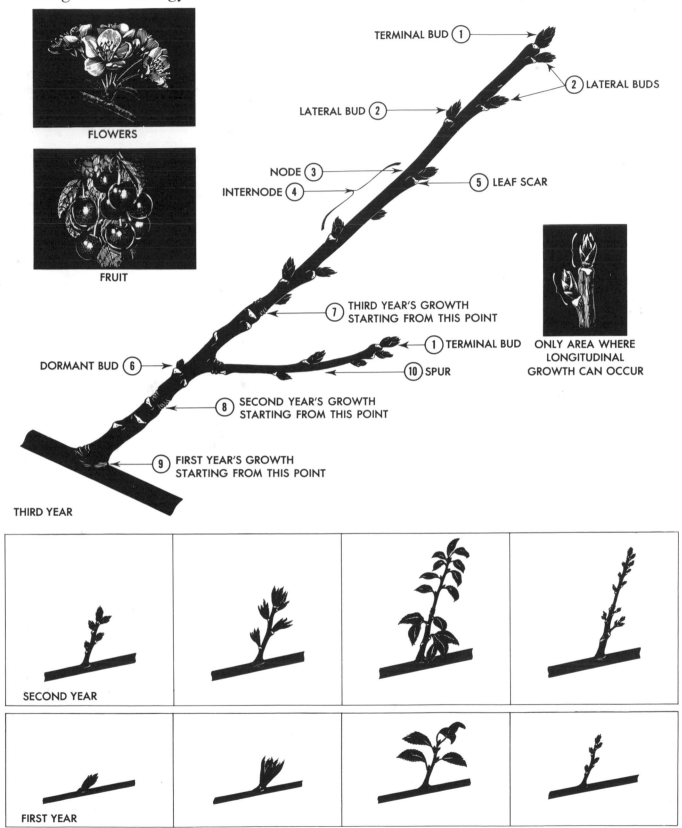

FLOWERS

FRUIT

TERMINAL BUD ①

② LATERAL BUDS

LATERAL BUD ②

NODE ③

INTERNODE ④

⑤ LEAF SCAR

⑦ THIRD YEAR'S GROWTH STARTING FROM THIS POINT

① TERMINAL BUD

⑩ SPUR

DORMANT BUD ⑥

⑧ SECOND YEAR'S GROWTH STARTING FROM THIS POINT

⑨ FIRST YEAR'S GROWTH STARTING FROM THIS POINT

THIRD YEAR

ONLY AREA WHERE LONGITUDINAL GROWTH CAN OCCUR

SECOND YEAR

FIRST YEAR

If other conditions are favorable, bud differentiation will start when the proper balance is reached. Some of the leaf buds will start to form flowers, at which time they normally fatten out and can be distinguished from those that do not change. Their position on the branch varies with each species, and can only be learned by close observation. Taking the peach as an example, observation will show that there are usually three buds at each node. The center one rarely differentiates, but if conditions are right the two side ones will become flower buds. The leaf buds are always present and will develop leaves whether or not the side buds are present or develop flowers.

Effects of Pruning

Now, when you snip off a leaf, cut a branch, pick flowers or fruit, what happens to the plant?

Let us make a couple of basic cuts on a hypothetical rose bush and see what occurs.

For our experiment, we select a mature, healthy, well-grown bush that normally grows to a height of 4 feet. At pruning time, we cut one of the strong outside stems 6 *inches* from the ground just above an outside bud. Cut another similar stem in the same way, but make the cut 3 *feet* from ground level. Let the balance of the bush remain at the normal 4-foot height. What happens?

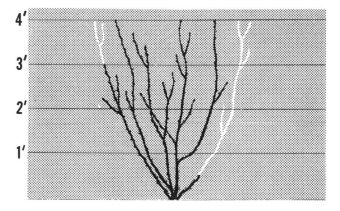

1. From the top bud on each stub, a new stem develops; but the buds farther down the stem remain inactive.

2. Each of the new stems grows to a height of 4 feet. The stem that grows out of the short stub thus grows 3½ feet, the one that develops from the lightly cut stub, only 1 foot.

3. The long, clean stems from the 6-inch stub produce fine roses of superior quality, but the weaker stems of the 3-foot stub produce a raft of meager blooms.

Let us take a closer look at these three phenomena and discover what bearing they may have on the techniques of pruning.

Bud Response to Pruning. When the top buds on each stub developed instead of the others, the rose bush

R. L. Hudson, Photo

Pruning can shape plants for special purposes. Elm and sycamore trees pruned annually to preserve park vista

was merely following a normal response. As a rule, the cutting back of a branch or limb affects only the buds in the immediate vicinity of the cut. It is not thoroughly understood why these buds remain dormant until the terminal or growing buds are removed, nor is it known exactly why the top buds are usually the only ones that start into growth, but it is generally conceded to be the retarding effect of certain plant hormones produced in the terminal growing point that prevents the growth of lateral buds.

We need not be concerned with the chemical processes involved. It is enough for us to know that practically every plant grown in the garden responds in this same manner. We can make use of this knowledge in many ways.

When a branch is cut to an outside bud, we can be reasonably sure that this top bud will make a new branch, which will grow out from the crown of the tree, and prevent crowding and criss-crossing. An injury or drying out of the stub may cause buds lower down to become dominant, and in the case of some trees, like the elm, severe heading will produce a veritable rash of shoots of equal vigor along many feet of the branches. Other trees, like the Lombardy poplar and some varieties of pears, have such a fastigiate habit that pruning has little effect on the crowding nature of the branches. Again, any tree grown against a high wall or a dense mass of other trees will be likely to grow from buds facing the source of light, whether they are the topmost ones or not. However,

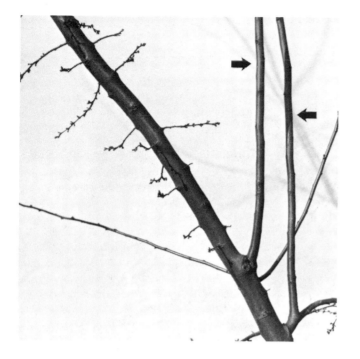

George Krebs, Photo

Watersprouts on plum tree caused by heading. Should have been summer pruned or tip pinched while small

these are the exceptions, and the general rule still holds true and is of great value to us in training our plants.

We can direct new growth to fill up bare spaces that develop from storm damage or from the removal of a large branch. A shrub or tree may be moulded to a marked extent by cutting at different lengths two branches of equal size and vigor. The longer and higher one will invariably become dominant, the degree of dominance depending on where the cut was made. The greater the difference in length, the greater will be the ultimate difference in their size.

Where prevailing winds or crowding have caused a plant to grow or lean heavily to one side, we may help balance the framework by severely pruning the heavy side and lightly thinning the weak side. This over-all working of the plant has far more effect than the immediate improvement in balance. It will actually divert some of the moisture and nutrients from the strong side of the tree to the weak side, as the root system attempts to re-establish its balance with the top. This generally requires more than one season to restore true bilateral symmetry, because the localized effect of the pruning will prevent as rapid an improvement as might be expected. Pruning on just one limb of a large shrub or tree will have very little noticeable effect on the remainder. As the percentage of the pruned part increases, so does the effect on the balance of the plant, although diffused and not readily recognized.

Control of Size. Remember that both of the newly developed stems on the rose bush caught up with the un-cut stems within a season. This illustrates the point mentioned above that all plants strive to reach or maintain their inherent size and shape, as modified by garden conditions.

Usually, this drive on the part of a plant is what keeps the gardener busiest with his pruning shears. Our hypothetical rose bush stops growing at 4 feet, but many shrubs and trees are not so considerate. A privet normally grows to a height of 15 to 20 feet—an inconvenient altitude for a hedge—and requires frequent pruning to keep it in scale. Some vines never seem to stop pushing out new growth. Many trees will inexorably grow as tall as a 10-story building if left to their own devices. The gardener has to prune with skill and knowledge if he is to keep his garden from engulfing him.

If a plant was properly chosen at the nursery and has room to develop naturally to its ultimate size, it should be pruned lightly. This will insure maximum growth and early productivity.

If a plant must be restrained to keep it within your garden's scale, it must be pruned heavily each year. It takes repeated hard pruning, in which almost as much wood is removed as is produced each year, to effect a dwarfing influence on the plant. Only when you have consistently removed enough wood to change the ratio of root system to leaf system, do you bring the size of the plant within bounds. Decreased foliage provides less food for the extension of the root system, and reduced root intake in turn supports less abundant foliage. However, a plant that has been dwarfed by pruning alone must be watched in succeeding years to prevent a gradual return to normal vigor. Many shrubs and some trees will revert rapidly if you relax vigilance.

Remember, always, that each species has its own response to, and need for, pruning. What is extremely heavy pruning to a cherry tree would be light pruning, indeed, to a peach tree. One warning should be given here. Severe pruning, after long neglect, will generally cause many weak and spindly growths to develop in some species, and thick, soft growths to start from dormant buds along the main branches in other species. The latter are called watersprouts and are a detriment to most trees and shrubs, although occasionally one can be used to fill an opening in the framework caused by storm or other injury. Their removal is an important part of summer pruning.

Rate of Growth. Our rose bush reacted to the two pruning cuts in another significant way: the short stub developed a long stem, the long stub broke out a short stem. One grew 3½ feet in a season, the other only 1 foot.

The rapid and abundant growth that developed from the short stub was due to the fact that there was only a small amount of old stem wood to be fed—one-eighth of the wood for which food was stored—and, being closer to the food supply, the new bud was fed more efficiently. On the other hand, the long stem had to draw nourishment for its 3 feet of wood, with its leaves and branchlets, in addition to the new growth. Moreover, the nutrients were drawn upward through old and less efficient plumbing.

Thus it appears that the harder you prune, the more abundant the response. This is usually true—up to a point. If a moderate portion of the plant is pruned heavily, the plant will be invigorated. The well-established root system will furnish the remaining buds a greatly increased supply of nutrients, by apportioning the same amount of food among a smaller number of buds, and the thinned foliage will receive more light and manufacture food more efficiently. However, if too much foliage is removed, the capacity of the plant to produce food is cut, and it begins to become dwarfed.

It was at one time customary to prune orchard trees severely, but this has been found to reduce the bearing capacity of some trees. Young trees are usually not cut back so severely as they used to be, nor are the unwanted branchlets along the stems removed so religiously as in the past. These are tip pinched or lightly cut back so that most of their leaves can continue producing carbohydrates.

Flower and Fruit Production. Of most interest to the gardener who is intent on growing colorful blooms is the floral response to the two pruning cuts. The short-stubbed rose branch produced large, long-stemmed flowers; the long-stubbed one yielded only small, short-stemmed blooms.

The first cut renewed the wood which will produce many fine roses; the second cut will leave a long, old stem that will gradually harden and deteriorate, until it finally ceases to produce blooming wood and will have to be removed.

The reasons for this are the same as those explained above. Simply stated, the food is apportioned among fewer growing points. Instead of being dispersed into three dozen roses, it is funneled into perhaps a dozen. As a result, the few well-nourished roses outdo the mass of half-starved ones.

The gardener learns from this experience that if he wants an abundance of small flowers for garden decoration, he should prune lightly and leave a lot of wood. If he wants large exhibition blooms for cutting, he should prune more severely and thin out a good portion of the old wood.

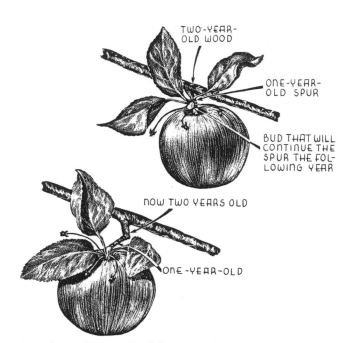

Age of wood from which fruit and flowers grow varies by species. For example, apples bear fruit on 1-year spurs

The same rules apply to the raising of fruit, since flowers turn to fruit (seed) if allowed to complete their cycle. So it is that the gardener who wants luscious peaches prunes his tree hard to concentrate the stored food in a smaller number of fruiting buds; but if he lets the tree follow its own inclinations, he will be rewarded with a wealth of small, bitter peaches.

Now, flowers and fruit are borne on wood of different ages, according to the species. Some flowers develop on new wood, some on year-old wood, some on two-year-old branches. This varies from plant to plant, and is discussed in more detail in later chapters.

Heading Back and Thinning Out

There are two basic pruning techniques, known as *heading* and *thinning*. *Heading* is cutting back branches

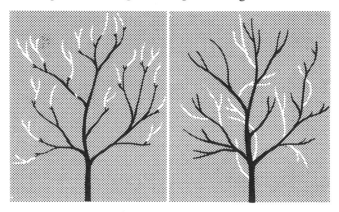

Heading back   *Thinning out*

to buds. This technique invariably leaves a stub, regardless of the age of the branch or the position of the cut. *Thinning* is the complete removal of branches back to a lateral or the main trunk. In the case of some shrubs, thinning also includes the cutting of stems to ground level. Some species require more heading and others require more thinning, which will also vary with the age of the subject. Heading produces a more bushy appearance because it usually increases the number of shoots and leaves per unit of space. Thinning gives a plant an open and natural appearance and encourages healthy new growths without the stubby effect caused by too much indiscriminate heading. In general practice both heading and thinning are used to some extent and the terms will be used freely in the descriptions of individual cases to follow.

Winter Pruning

The time when we pruned that rose bush can have a decisive effect on its response. The major portion of the pruning tasks have traditionally been done in the dormant period of winter and early spring. The gardener usually has more time available at this season, and most plants respond more favorably then than later.

Deciduous and partly deciduous materials may be studied and pruned to better advantage after the leaves have fallen. Mature, bearing fruit trees are, of course, pruned while dormant. Dormant pruning is becoming less and less severe as a better understanding of plant physiology becomes general among the commercial growers. This is especially true in the young orchards that have not come into bearing.

Summer Pruning

Summer pruning is a particularly valuable technique to use in the early training of both fruit and ornamental trees, and can be used on many broadleaved evergreen shrubs throughout their life. Deciduous shrubs should seldom be included in this operation as their pruning requirements are quite different. The deciduous shrub has a much shorter period in which to manufacture food, and any considerable amount of summer pruning (loss of leaves) would seriously weaken the plant. However, the too-vigorous canes can be tipped without danger.

Pinching might be a better name for the process, as most of it can be done with the thumb nail or a light pair of shears. Grape or thinning shears are obtainable which are excellent for the purpose. Summer pruning should always be done early in the year when the new shoots have made but 3 or 4 inches growth. At this stage, the shoots not needed for branches can have their tips

pinched out easily. This will throw all the strength of the plant into the branches which will form the framework we desire. The pinched shoots will shade the bark of the tree and continue to produce plant foods without compet-

Pinch above a bud

ing with the main branches. The first pinching back should be followed in about 6 weeks by a close examination to discover if any new growths, that are undesirable, need to be checked.

Two or three seasons of this type of light summer pruning will greatly reduce the amount of dormant pruning and will produce a shapely tree, without the stubby and knobby branches so frequently seen where they have been allowed to grow unchecked for one or more seasons before heading. This will also control any possible watersprouts before they become large enough to disturb the pattern of branches that we have obtained by careful pruning.

Summer pruning is especially desirable for trees like the maple, which bleed badly if pruned in late winter or spring, although this trouble can also be avoided by pruning in the fall. It is best for the conifers, which should be lightly pinched or sheared back while the new growths are short and soft. Conifers should never be pruned back to the old wood. Very few of them will break well from hardened stems, especially on the lower branches.

Summer pruning is preferable for spring-blooming shrubs and trees, as dormant pruning would remove the flower buds and little or no bloom would result. When the flowers are used for cutting and/or the pruning is effected immediately after the blooming period, the physiological effect is much the same as dormant pruning.

Late summer pruning, in which large sections of the new twigs and their leaves would have to be removed, is not to be recommended. It robs the plant of much-needed food production and storage facilities and seriously weakens it.

CHAPTER 3

Pruning Tools and Their Use

There are several firms making pruning tools, either as a specialty or as a side line of general hardware business. These firms control various patents and market a wide array of competitive products. Each type of pruning shears, pole shears, or pruning saw has its following, and it is impossible to give exact specifications for *your* particular needs. Each product, in its price class, has undoubted merit and can be purchased with confidence from reputable seed or hardware dealers.

One word of advice. You get only the quality for which you are willing to pay. Do not bargain hunt for pruning tools. Buy only the best obtainable. Good steel is expensive, but cheap tools are far more expensive in the long run. A good pair of shears, with reasonable care, will last the home gardener a lifetime, if used properly for the work for which they were designed. An inferior tool will not hold an edge, and will spring out of shape and become unusable just when you need it most. The welfare of your plants depends upon whether or not you use tools that make sharp, clean cuts, with a minimum of bruising.

Your Kit of Tools

If your garden is small and contains but few hard-wooded plants, your pruning kit can also be small. It is actually possible to do all the pruning required in such a garden with a pair of good, medium weight, hand-pruning shears. It adds to one's pleasure, however, to have a light pair for summer pruning and flower removal and a heavy pair for winter pruning and heavy work.

There are two principal types of hand-pruning shears widely used at the present time. The older and more familiar type, still the favorite of most professionals, is the

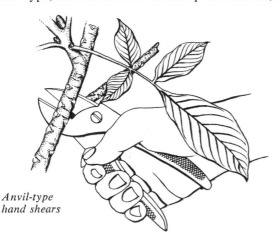

Anvil-type hand shears

drop-forged shears that have a tool-steel cutting edge and a thicker hook that works with a scissors-like action. When in good condition and properly used, this tool makes a clean, close cut. The other type is of anvil construction and has a perfectly straight-edged blade opposite a flat bed of soft metal. Its frame is generally of rolled

Drop-forged pruning shears

steel or aluminum and is much lighter than the drop-forged tool of equal capacity. Because of its light weight, it appeals to many home gardeners. However, some professionals contend that this type is more likely to bruise the branch, and they also claim that it is harder to make a close cut with it.

It is with hesitancy that the hedge shears are mentioned, because of the assorted pruning crimes that are committed with this excellent tool. But obviously, if hedges are a feature of your property, you must have them. You have the choice between hand-operated or electric-driven shears. Either will do the job efficiently.

An ordinary single-jointed lopper will cut branches up to an inch, or an inch and a quarter, in diameter. Sometimes, even with branches of this size, you run into tough cutting. For such conditions, there is a heavy-duty lopping shears available with a patented power slot built

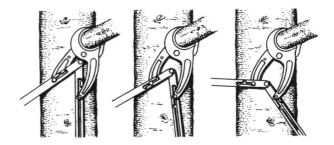

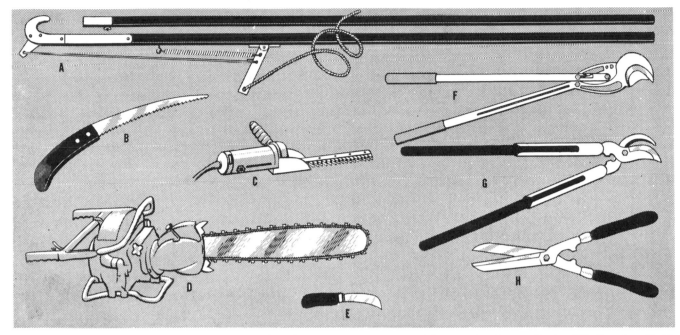

Specialized tools for pruning kit: (A) Extension Pruner *for reaching high branches; (B)* Pruning Saw *for cutting thick branches; (C)* Electric Hedge Shears *for quick, efficient hedge trimming; (D)* Power Saw *(rentable in many areas) for cutting heavy limbs; (E)* Pruning Knife *for light, all-around use; (F)* Heavy Duty Lopper *for branches to 1½ inches; (G)* Lopper *for branches to 1 inch; (H)* Hedge Shears, *the basic hand tool for hedges*

in. If you need more cutting power than you get from the normal position, you simply shift the handles to the next power.

To keep your lopping shears cutting sharp and clean, put a drop of oil on the bearing occasionally. Sharpen the cutting blade on a whetstone from time to time. If the shears tear when they cut, see if you can tighten them. If you can't, they may have sprung and are no longer a fit pruning tool.

You shouldn't run into much trouble with your lopping shears if you remember two rules. Never force the tool on branches too large, and never allow the cutting end to touch the ground. Dirt can ruin the bearing.

Use the pruning saw for branches which the loppers won't take. One popular type of pruning saw has a curved blade, tapering to a point for use in close quarters, with about seven teeth to the inch. Biting on the pull stroke, it cuts fast. There is a folding pruning saw with a handle that folds over to protect the teeth. You can carry this saw in your pocket.

Another useful device is the extension pruner that gets at high, hard-to-reach branches. You can cut branches up to an inch in diameter with it. For bigger branches too high to reach, use a pruning saw on an extension pole.

We can't leave a discussion of pruning equipment without at least mentioning pneumatic pruners. They work by air pressure, cutting off branches up to an inch and a quarter in diameter, with just the press of a button. The pruner attaches to a compressor with an air hose; the compressor can be driven by a gasoline engine or a tractor power take-off. Models are available which can be run off small garden tractors. These pruners have the disadvantage of being quite expensive and requiring scaffolding for the operator to stand on.

Pruning-Wound Dressing

While not a tool, a very valuable addition to your pruning kit is a can or bucket of tree wound compound. There are several proprietary brands on the market that are much less bother and but slightly more expensive than home-made mixtures advocated in the past. They are scientifically prepared and may be used freely without fear of any toxic properties.

Many orchardists prefer a mixture of white lead and *raw* linseed oil to which they generally add some bordeaux powder. This is considered to be a cheap and absolutely foolproof wound covering. Your choice then is between a black or a white compound. The black is usually more unobtrusive.

Tools for Large Properties

The large property or woodland summer home with many trees will have need for a still greater collection of pruning equipment.

A large, one- or two-man cross-cut saw is a necessity for sawing up large branches; and a heavy duty pruning saw will be needed for large stubs. Both electric and gasoline driven saws are obtainable, using either the drag-saw or the chain-saw principle. The gasoline-driven, aluminum-frame chain saw leads the field in this department. All of these power tools are great time-savers and labor-savers. They may be rented in some localities.

A long-handled double-bitted axe is required for thinning woodland areas; and a sharp, light hand-axe is useful in many ways.

It is inevitable that some climbing must be done on occasion, but it is strongly advised that professional tree men be engaged for this task. It is dangerous work requiring special skill and aptitude, and it should not be attempted by an amateur. If the staff on a large place includes a man young enough and experienced enough to attempt such work, he must be provided with a good safety belt and sufficient new, high quality rope to protect both himself and the tree and underplanting in which he is working.

A word of warning: There are many itinerant, self-styled tree men who can do serious damage, both to your trees and property, and to themselves. Only men of known experience should be trusted in your priceless trees, and you should insist that they show proof of insurance, covering both accident and liability.

Care of Tools

Cutting tools should be kept sharp at all times to prevent bruising the cut branches.

The average amateur usually has trouble sharpening these tool-steel edges, and he finds the set and filing of saws especially baffling. Many fine tools are unintentionally rendered ineffectual by poor sharpening technique, and it is strongly advised that this task be assigned to an expert. Every town and city has at least one good tool sharpener patronized by carpenters and gardeners.

Prevent rust from forming by wiping tools with an oiled rag after use and by keeping the working parts well lubricated. This will prevent shears from sticking and will allow the spring to open the jaws of the tool.

Making the Cut

The hand shears do the major part of the pruning in the average garden. If of good design and quality, and if kept in proper condition, they will make smooth, clean cuts in all material from soft green shoots up to mature limbs one-half to three-fourths of an inch in diameter.

The shears should be grasped firmly and the branch to be cut should be inserted deeply into the jaws. This prevents slipping, provides more cutting leverage, and helps to prevent the springing of the blades. Never twist and turn the shears while making a cut. This will bruise the

branch and leave a ragged cut, and it will very soon spring the blades out of alignment, making the tool worse than useless.

Keep the thin cutting blade toward the portion of the branch that is to be left on the bush or tree. When possible, it is a good habit to make all cuts on the side of the plant to your left as you face it. Move clockwise around the plant as you prune, and the shears will always be in a natural, comfortable position. Of course, in thick shrubberies or with plants grown against a fence or wall, this is not always convenient.

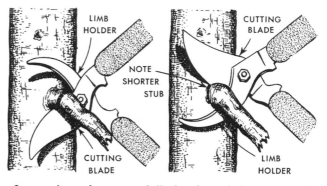

Larger branches, especially hardwooded ones, can be more easily cut if the shears are held sideways in an up-and-down position parallel to the main branch. This makes a clean cut with less danger of springing the blades. In any case, a *slight* pressure with the free hand on the part to be removed, in a way to open the cut, will materially aid the operation.

Where to Cut

When heading back or shortening the branches of shrubs or young trees, cuts should be carefully made just above a good healthy bud. In older trees we have already learned that drying out or crowding will sometimes cause other than the top buds to take the lead. Bud placement should be ignored in such cases. With most plants of an upright nature, the top bud should be an outside one, so that the new branch will have room to develop without interfering with other branches and will keep the center of the plant open. In the case of plants which are inclined to weep or droop, it might be desirable to cut to an inside bud to get a more upright branching habit. The photograph shows the proper angle and position of the pruning cut. In the colder climates, a little more wood is left beyond the bud in winter pruning. This helps to prevent the drying effect of the cold from reaching the bud.

Use the lopping shears for the larger branches, as they have the added advantage of increasing your reach. They are also very useful for cutting sucker growth and for the thinning of barberries and other thorny shrubs and vines. The principle of making the cut is exactly as de-

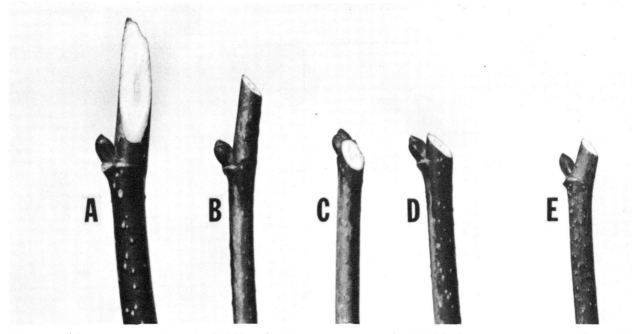

Proper and improper pruning cuts. (A) Too slanting, exposes too much heartwood. (B) Too long, will cause dieback of stub. (C) Too short, will interfere with bud growth. (D) Ideal cut, starts opposite base of bud and slants up toward top of bud. (E) Slightly longer cut practiced in cold climates to prevent drying out of bud

scribed above for the hand shears. Still larger cuts and extremely tough woods require the use of the heavy-duty lopping shears or the pruning saw. Any branch too large to be comfortably supported with the free hand, when using the pruning saw, should be stubbed off at least 6 inches from the finished cut and then resawed at the proper place. This prevents splitting and bark stripping which could seriously damage a tree. Proper and improper cuts and the result of each are shown in the photograph on the next page.

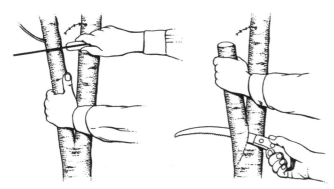

First cut removes limb; second, the stub

Note that the finish cuts are not made tight up against the main branch or trunk. So many warnings are given about leaving stubs that many gardeners are inclined to make their finish cuts flush with the main trunk. This practice exposes an unnecessary amount of heartwood and retards the healing process. It is better to leave a slight shoulder and to cut on an angle that will slant away from the trunk. This exposes a round or slightly oval section of heartwood in the maximum healing area. These cuts should always be painted with a wound compound if they are more than 2 inches in diameter.

Removing Large Limbs

Occasionally a large limb must be removed entirely. The process is essentially the same as outlined above, but it requires special equipment in most cases. This is work for the professional. He has the proper tools and the knowledge of rigging his ropes in the correct manner to prevent breakage and damage to surrounding features in the garden.

For those who have trees that stand in the open and who wish to attempt the task themselves, the following hints will be in order. Cut off as many as possible of the outer branches from the limb to be removed. The weight of a large branch with all of its twigs and leaves is tremendous, and it can be a very dangerous force if improperly handled. Even experts sometimes underestimate this weight; and unless ropes and lines are new or in good condition, accidents can easily happen. The stripping of the branch also removes the springing force of the tip. Many branches, when dropped from a tree intact, will fall into a coiled position and then rebound for many feet, often in the direction of the operator. Many ladders

Results of proper and improper removal of large limbs. (A) Cuts properly made are healing satisfactorily. (B) Improper cut has left stub that can never heal. Note the lichens growing from the stub and the absence of cambium tissue

have been knocked out from under surprised gardeners with painful results.

After the limb is lightened and stubbed back, a support should be given to the end of the limb nearest the trunk. This is usually a rope thrown over a higher branch and tied around the limb to be removed, about 3 feet from the finish cut. This allows room for the rough under-cut and top-cut to be made about 2 feet from the trunk. Caution should again be exercised so the limb does not kick

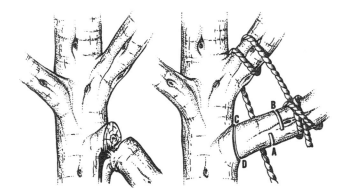

If a heavy limb is not properly cut, it is certain to split, and rip off the bark when it falls. Proper technique requires three cuts: downcut at B, upcut at A for removal of limb. Stub can then be cut off with a single cut from C to D. Free end of limb is supported by rope. The stub should also be supported to prevent ripping the bark

back against the operator or his ladder. Be sure to protect the branch on which your line is supported so that the weight and friction will not damage the bark.

After lowering the cut limb with the rope, retie the rope to the 2-foot stub so that a smooth, even cut can be made without danger of stripping the bark. Even a 2-foot stub can be heavy enough to rip off a huge section of bark and leave a wound which may take years to heal. It is far better to support the stub and cut it clear through with one cut, rather than to attempt to undercut again, because the undercut is unlikely to match the top-cut exactly.

Protection of Cut Surfaces. This was discussed above, but must be emphasized particularly in connection with the removal of large limbs. There is nothing known that will hasten the healing of a wound in a plant. A wound covering merely protects the heartwood until the cambium layer can grow out over the cut surface and seal it. Broken branches and improperly cut limbs heal slowly, if at all, and are a ready entrance point for insect pests, diseases, and dry rot. Large cuts should be inspected regularly and additional coats of protective covering should be applied, when needed, until the wound is entirely healed. The various stages of healing are shown in the photograph picturing proper limb removal. Properly made cuts will heal evenly and rapidly, in most species, and no other care is required.

CHAPTER 4. Evergreen and Deciduous Shrubs

In every garden, shrubs play an essential role. They give screening, soften architectural lines or define garden design, provide contrast in color and texture. How well they perform often depends upon the gardener's skill with the shears and his understanding of the simple pruning needs of his plant materials.

I. Evergreen Shrubs

In this manual the term "evergreen shrub" will denote broadleaved evergreen species. It is recognized that "evergreens" will mean conifers to readers in regions where the broadleaved materials are in an extreme minority. However, we wish to include the shrub-sized conifers along with the tree types in a section of their own.

Along the west coast of America, as well as in the southern states, broadleaved evergreens predominate, almost to the exclusion of deciduous materials. California, in particular, is endowed with a climate which allows the widest selection of this class of material, and the plant list at the end of the chapter contains the names of many plants, commonly grown in the West, that are completely unknown as outdoor garden plants in the North and East. By the same token, many of the deciduous species, which are the mainstay of gardens in the frost belts, are little used in warmer climates. We will endeavor to explain the basic principles so that everyone, regardless of his location, can profit from the use of this book, no matter which type of plant predominates in his garden.

The pruning of rhododendrons is described in a separate chapter, so this section will be of interest mainly to those living in areas with a minimum temperature well above zero.

How Much Pruning Needed?

Broadleaved evergreens as a class *require* less pruning than deciduous plant materials. It is generally not necessary to prune many of them to induce flowering or fruiting. We should always make this distinction when considering a particular plant. Does it *need* to be pruned? What is to be accomplished by pruning? If no obvious benefit is to be derived from the operation, do not prune broadleaved evergreens at all. To prune automatically all of one's shrubs annually, because it seems the thing to do, or because of advice or an article explaining how it is to be done, is patently foolish. All directions given herein are for shrubs that *need* pruning.

Broadleaved evergreens suffer the most from improper

pruning, and are far too frequently the victims of the hedge-shears operator. There are several reasons why this is true. Nursery stock is commonly sold from small containers at a very reasonable price. This encourages overplanting even beyond the gardener's natural desire to have as wide a selection of plant materials as possible, and beyond the capacity of his pruning shears to cope with the crowding growth. Lack of knowledge of the new plant's mature size and habit also contributes to overcrowding. The reluctance with which the owner will remove a sufficient number of plants, to permit the natural development of those that remain, leaves but one alternative: constant heavy, outside pruning, heading back or shearing. The summer pruning mentioned earlier will aid this effort as will the thinning back to the weaker laterals. To do none of these things would result in an impenetrable mass that could only be tolerated in a wild or woodland garden where natural forces ultimately thin in their ruthless way.

Another reason for improper pruning is the practice of hiring jobbing gardeners by the hour and expecting them to do a complete job in the shortest possible time. Good, careful, scientific pruning takes from three to four times as long as hedge-shear pruning. If you hire a gardener to do your pruning, first learn how the various plants in your collection should be pruned, be sure that the gardener knows how, and then allow him sufficient time to do the job properly.

1. Slow-Growing Shrubs

We can roughly divide the broadleaved evergreen shrubs into two groups. Group One contains those species

Rhododendron

and varieties that normally have a slow, even, and compact growth habit. Most of their growth originates from terminal buds, and the foliage forms a dome of green with but few leaves in the interior of the plant. Along the West Coast many plants are grown that follow this habit of growth. Among them are the hybrid rhododendron, the evergreen viburnums, and the veronicas, or hebes as they are now properly called.

This group requires very little heading back. Only the occasional branch that outgrows the rest of the shrub needs to be shortened. This can best be done by pinching out the tips during the period of active growth. All that then remains to be done is to remove the weak, dead, diseased and criss-crossing branches from the center of the shrub. Pruning of this type has little influence on the plant's growth, neither stimulating it nor retarding it; therefore, it may be done at any time during the year. Late fall is an ideal time because pruning then admits more air and light into the center of the plant during the dark, damp days of winter, and it exposes the hiding place of insect pests and dormant fungus spores. Shrubs that require spraying are easier to spray, and better coverage of the spray material is obtained.

A quick follow-up pruning in spring will remove branches broken by storms or nipped by a hard, late frost. Do not be in too great a hurry to prune out frost damage. It has been proven many times that it is better to wait until new growth is well started before removing seemingly dead branches.

2. Fast-Growing Shrubs

The second group of broadleaved evergreens consists of those that, more or less, follow the growth habits of the deciduous shrubs and are pruned in a similar manner.

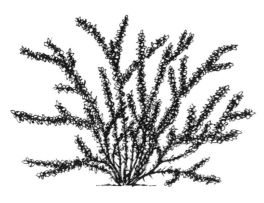

Berberis

They throw strong sucker growths from the roots and strong laterals from the branches. These laterals divert the water and nutrients away from the ends of the main branches, and their weight and vigor force these branches down. This results in a straggly shrub that is constantly increasing in diameter; and, unless curbed, it becomes a hopeless jungle that will smother all of its more fas-

tidious neighbors. Of course, well-placed laterals may well add to the beauty of the plant, and a few are sometimes retained at the time of pruning. The escallonias and berberis are good examples of this group. They require heavy and ruthless pruning, unless our gardens are to resemble the jungles from which these plants came.

The following technique has been developed from years of experience with this class of material, and it is recommended to the beginner until a personal method has been evolved. The main requirements of the method are a willingness to devote ample time and care to the task and the courage to cut boldly but purposefully into a fine shrub. Remember that it is only by removing *live* tissue that the shrub is strengthened in the tissues that remain. The latent or dormant growth buds on the lower stems and branches are present in amazing numbers and their vitality is remarkable. While it is not recommended except in extreme cases, most of this group may actually be cut down entirely, to just above ground level, and they will still break out quickly and regain their former size in a surprisingly short time. Therefore, if the plant is in a normal, healthy condition, no fears need be entertained for the life of the shrub, even when it is severely thinned and headed back.

Step 1. Take your hand-pruning shears, lopping shears, and small pruning saw into the garden. With the hand shears shorten back all long, ungainly shoots and obtain the rough contour of the shrub by cutting back all current year's growth to short spurs of from 4 to 6 inches in length. If the habit of the plant is upright, cut to outside buds. If it is inclined to droop and the branches are

horizontal, cut to an inside bud which would be a "top" bud in this case. If, as is usually the case, there are three or more terminal shoots of about equal strength, remove the center ones, leaving the two that are lowest on the older growth. If the new growth consists of strong laterals down the old branch, select a couple of well-spaced branches to remain and remove the rest. This will make well-spread forks and relieve the congestion and criss-crossing of the new shoots. After going completely around the shrub in this manner, you will find that it still retains a natural, distinctive shape, closely following its original contour and only a little larger than it was the previous year.

Step 2. Now you are able to move in closer and, in the case of older shrubs, you will switch to your lopping shears. Start at the ground level and remove all branches that have been forced down to the ground. They are gen-

erally weak and starved, conceal garden pests, and make cultivating and weeding difficult. Then proceed up through the shrub, removing weak growths, dead wood, broken or split branches, criss-crossed branches, and diseased or insect-infested parts. The shrub is beginning to look rather bare, but your task is not yet finished.

Step 3. With the pruning saw you now remove, clear to the base, as many of the *oldest* growths as possible, while still retaining the shape of your plant. Of course, you are removing several of the branches that you have just pruned, but it is well worth the slight additional effort.

Your previous work has made the framework of the plant plainly visible, thus preventing the removal of large branches that you can see are important to the shape of the plant. It is far better to make two or three cuts in removing a large limb than to cut it out all at once and discover, too late, that a part of it was needed. Still at least

one-third of the old, woody stems should be removed annually.

This operation provides the space and admits the necessary light and air for the sturdy new growths that will keep renewing your shrub indefinitely. It is possible in this way to keep vigorous, youthful-appearing shrubs for many years past their normal life expectancy, thus cutting down the labor and expense of replacements.

Now, this is an admittedly severe method of pruning, reserved for those plants of an age or condition requiring it. Along the entire Pacific coastline and in the deep South, the climatic and moisture conditions favor vegetative growth to a degree unheard of elsewhere in this country. Gardeners who live in areas where growth is more restrained will modify the severity of pruning accordingly. Such a pruning in alternate years, or even every third year, might be all that is required to obtain the same results that annual pruning provides in the coastal fog belt.

Many shrubs, such as pyracantha, need only occasional pruning for control and shaping. Flowered wood thinned

Hedges and Formal Plants

Hedges are not so popular as they used to be when land was cheap and plentiful and labor costs were low. However, there are places where nothing else will do as well or seem as fitting in the garden picture. In the smaller and more intimate gardens of today it is essential that the hedge be trim and well cared for.

A hedge must be pruned from the day it is planted for as long as it is in existence. This form of pruning is called trimming, shearing, or clipping; and it is in performing this task that the hedge-shears take their rightful place. The moderately-priced electric hedge trimmer is rapidly taking over this work and it is a splendid labor saver. It also encourages the gardener to trim more often, which results in a thicker and more beautiful hedge. Most hedges should be trimmed at least twice a year, and three or even four times would be better.

At planting time, hedge plants such as privet and berberis should be cut off evenly a few inches from the ground, depending upon their size and shape. Allow the new growth to develop for the first growing season to encourage strong root action, and then again cut back hard to within 4 to 6 inches of the previous cut. Never attempt to establish the desired height the first season. It would only result in top-heavy plants with poorly furnished stems.

As new growth develops, trim back to within a few inches of the preceding cut. This usually causes side branches to develop and fill in the bottom of the hedge. Such growth is possible only while the plants are young and are being severely headed back. Once the plants have reached a few feet in height, they are almost impossible to fill in at the base.

When the bottom and side branches have grown to sufficient length, they too must be trimmed back. As the width of a hedge is generally much less than the height, succeeding side clippings should be made very close to the previous cuts. The sides of the hedge may be straight up and down, but the health of the plants is improved if they slope in at the top. Under no circumstances should the top be wider than the base.

The last trimming should be done in late summer. If left until late fall, the new shoots will not have time to

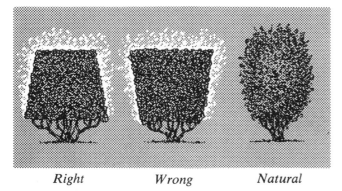

Right   *Wrong*   *Natural*

harden and will be highly susceptible to frost damage, which in turn results in die-back.

The finest hedges are those that utilize the inherent shape of the plant and are allowed to develop in an informal manner. Neatness and uniformity can be maintained by occasional light shearing, but the ideal maintenance would be the use of hand shears to shorten back

any branches that grow too strongly. This can be done at any time of the year and in such a way that the cuts are hidden and the plants escape the artificial bobbed look too often encountered.

Many fine shrubs in the lists make excellent hedge materials in the milder climates. Where hardiness is essential, the conifers become the leading contenders. They are usually benefited by the removal of the tips, to induce bushiness. If prevented from making a strong leader, conifers will retain their bottom branches indefinitely.

II. Deciduous Shrubs

The plants that lose their leaves each fall are, for the most part, extremely hardy and make up the bulk of the plantings in all sections where temperatures drop below zero in winter. In the West and the South, more and more discriminating gardeners are introducing some of the better deciduous shrubs and trees into their plantings. These are a great comfort in the borderline areas where an occasional severe winter will wipe out a great many broadleaved evergreens.

In mild climates many deciduous shrubs miss the essential chilling necessary to make their buds start growth normally in the spring, which causes irregular leafing and shy blooming. The lack of severe frosts or freezes will usually prevent characteristic fall colors. Summer pruning can be important in these areas, but is seldom practiced. As explained earlier, this consists of merely pinching the tips of the shoots, and the method can be used quite generally except in the case of terminal bloomers, such as the viburnums. This tip pinching has an effect on the ripening of the wood and the setting of buds. If most of the branches have just the top 2 or 3 inches removed toward the end of summer, tip pinching does not have the effect of forcing new vegetative growth. The long growing season and the mild, wet winters do not favor dormancy. Plants that are resting, fully ripened and dormant in the more rigorous climates, sometimes go into the open winter in full, soft growth. Thus any practice by which we are able to hasten the ripening of the wood is very worthwhile.

When to Prune

The temperament and garden habits of the individual gardener have a good deal of bearing on the time of pruning. Many gardeners, and good ones, too, feel that pruning should be one grand clean-up of the entire planting. This is done but once a year and is a major operation. Everything gets "cut back." Roses, vines, trees and

BEFORE: A weigela branch loaded with spent flowering wood, suckers, weak stems, sturdy unflowered shoots

AFTER: Same weigela branch after pruning. Spent wood and weak stems thinned out, remaining shoots not headed

shrubs, both deciduous and evergreen, are treated at the same time and in the same manner. This practice must be discouraged.

Obviously, the proper time to prune a tea rose could not possibly be the right time to prune a deutzia, which bears its flowers in late spring on mature wood. Winter and spring pruning are usually responsible for dissatisfaction with the flowering of deciduous shrubs. Not only are many of the flowering buds removed, but the shrub, when growth resumes, is likely to make a heavy vegetative growth at the expense of flowering wood. In the flurry of activity occasioned by spring gardening fever on the first warm sunny day, many beautiful sprays of flowers die unborn.

So, here again we divide our subjects into two groups. Group One contains the spring-flowering species and Group Two those that bloom in summer and fall.

1. Spring-Flowering Species. These shrubs are the species and varieties that bloom on new wood produced *before* the deciduous period. The one safe and sure rule for pruning this group is *prune immediately after flowering.* The free use of cut sprays for indoor decoration can provide an important part of the pruning, but rarely is it sufficient. A good many stems are unsuitable for floral cuttings, and they are the very ones that should be removed as soon as the garden display is over. Just after flowering, the shrub is in excellent condition for pruning. At this time, the roots are pushing, cuts heal quickly, and food that would have gone into the strain of seed production is released for the production of sound, strong wood and dormant buds for next year's display. In most cases the dead branches are more easily identified

at this season. Anyone who has tried to prune a deciduous, shrubby lonicera before growth starts in the spring will appreciate the advantage of this timing.

Proceed exactly as described above for Group Two of the broadleaved evergreens (page 22). Be sure your tools are sharp. Cut at the proper place and at the proper angle, as described and illustrated in Chapter Three.

In the West and South partial dormancy is responsible, to a large extent, for a condition that has bothered many gardeners, especially those who have previously gardened in the North and East. It is also troublesome to those who try to garden by eastern or English books and magazines. In areas of fully ripened wood, frozen soils, and blankets of snow, it is common practice to cut many shrubs entirely to the ground or to very short stumps. Then ashes or loam are heaped over the roots and topped off with straw or branches. Of course, in the mild climates the covering is omitted, but the heavy pruning is sometimes effected with the result that when the time comes for the shrubs to burst into glorious life, they are found dead or in an exceedingly weakened condition. This is especially true of the softer and more tender subjects, such as buddleja and leonotis. The reason is clear. Without the extreme cold, the roots are still active and busy supplying food to an only partly dormant plant. The return of plant food from leaf and stem for the support of the root system through the winter months has not yet been completed. The sudden and severe shock of the heavy pruning weakens the plant and may make it more vulnerable to diseases.

It is far better to use moderation and to rejuvenate over a period of two or three seasons, as outlined above. In the case of the buddleja and leonotis and shrubs of a similar nature that bloom only on new wood, it is better to let them go through the winter untouched. Then, as growth starts in the spring, they may be cut as severely as desired, with comparatively little risk of fatality.

This is also the best time to cut willows and dogwoods back to the ground. They have supplied their share of winter color, with their bright twigs and branches, and our purpose now is to obtain a fresh crop of new shoots for the next winter. Of course, this only applies to those species grown solely for their brightly colored new growths.

2. Summer- and Fall-Blooming Species. This group contains species and varieties that bloom in summer and fall, on the current year's growth. These may be pruned any time after leaf fall and before the start of new growth in the spring. In the colder sections, or with shrubs that are inclined to freeze back, the spring pruning is to be preferred. The same technique is followed as with the spring-flowering types.

During this period, the plant is bare of leaves and its framework is plainly visible. The complete dormancy of the branches may confuse the beginner as to their comparative age and vigor, but a close inspection of the bark will generally disclose a distinct difference between the old and new wood. Once the new growth has started, it should be allowed to grow unchecked, because tip pinching or summer pruning will prevent formation of flowers.

Digest of Pruning Requirements

The following section lists most of the shrubs that one may expect to find in the general nurseries of the continental United States. Specialty nurseries, arboretums and private collections contain many other plants that cannot be dealt with in a manual intended primarily for the amateur and home gardener.

Many fine books are available that describe in full detail the merits, hardiness, use, and cultural requirements of most of the listed plants. As this handbook is restricted to pruning methods and techniques, the list must, of necessity, contain only brief and terse advice. It is strongly advised that the preceding text be carefully read and understood before you attempt to use these lists. As soon as basic knowledge is acquired, a quick reference to the brief notes that follow will supply all the clues needed to proceed with the pruning of an unfamiliar shrub.

In California, there is little merit to the advice sometimes given to prune all deciduous plants while dormant. The reason advanced is that the shrubs grow so large and fast that it is impossible to do a good job without damage to the plant unless the pruning is done during dormancy. This is excellent chamber of commerce publicity for out-of-state consumption, but of doubtful value to the home gardener, especially a beginner. Properly trained, thinned, and pruned shrubs will never get so dense and intertangled that they cannot be worked on at the proper time. A light thinning and tidying up during dormancy is always in order in any climate, but throughout most of the West regular pruning of all spring-blooming deciduous shrubs should be done immediately after flowering.

Pruning, especially in the ornamental field, has no hard and fast rules. Words and even pictures can only suggest methods and cannot be slavishly followed. No two plants grow exactly alike any more than two people look exactly alike.

May we emphasize that the following pruning instructions indicate what *may* be done, not what *must* be done. You are the only judge of that. Plants that require pruning as a condition for good bloom or fruit or long life are so noted. It is extremely important to know how much cutting a plant can stand without serious damage when conditions demand unusual treatment. This is indicated in many cases.

Terms Used. In the abbreviated text that follows, certain terms are frequently repeated. "Habit" refers to the natural growth pattern that the shrub tends to follow. "Train" indicates the garden use for which the shrub is usually trained. In this connection, "specimen" is an individual shrub, grown for ornament. "Prune" refers to the shrub's basic pruning requirements, if any.

Best time for pruning is indicated under "Mild" for areas with little or no frost, "Cold" for areas where freezing is the rule. The fine points of timing must be determined by experience in your own locality. The preceding text has indicated what the response of a plant will be to pruning at different seasons.

It should be understood that a listed plant that "requires no pruning" must have dead wood, broken or criss-crossing branches, and diseased portions removed as soon as discovered. This is routine for every living plant in the garden. The term "training only" applies to a few shrubs that require a helping hand while forming the framework that will be the permanent support for the millions of leaves and flowers of the future. After this framework is established, pruning can usually be discontinued entirely unless control of size or shape is necessary.

"Cutting to the ground" means just that. Some writers tell exactly how many inches of stub should be left on each species. We do not condone the practice of leaving stubs. Practically all plants that are able to break from stubs will just as readily sprout from ground level or just beneath it. This produces a clean-limbed specimen, superior in every way to a shrub that has developed from a mass of short stubs that have accumulated through the years.

"Cutting to spurs" is quite another matter. This means the heading back of a *lateral* branch, that is young, strong and well-placed, to a good bud near the parent branch. It is used for wood renewal.

Species names are not used unless a species requires a different kind or degree of pruning from the rest of the genus to which it belongs. Some genera are quite uniform, but others contain many variations.

Abelia

Habit: Compact, arching. *Train:* Specimen, mass, hedge. *Prune:* Thin out brushy wood that has flowered. Preserve natural form. Tip new growth to control size. Will stand severe pruning even to ground. Mild: Fall. Cold: Spring.

Abutilon   *Flowering maple*

Habit: Thin, straggling. *Train:* Specimen, wall shrub. *Prune:* Head back to strong wood to keep plant compact and self-supporting. Mild: Fall or spring.

Acacia (shrubby types)

Habit: Weak, sprawling, rapid. *Train:* Specimen large informal hedge, clipped standards. *Prune:* Head back hard to prevent leggy and sprawling habit. Will stand either shearing or hard pruning. Mild: Any time, after flowering for blossoming types.

Acanthopanax pentaphyllus   *Five-leaved aralia*

Habit: Neat. *Train:* Specimen. *Prune:* Prune while dormant for training only.

Adenocarpus   *Canary Island lupine*

Habit: Loose, sprawling. *Train:* Specimen, wall plant, hedge. *Prune:* Lightly head to remove spent flowers. Can stand heavy pruning. Mild: After flowering.

Amelanchier   *Service-berry, June-berry, Shadbush*

Habit: Open, arching. *Train:* Specimen, copse. *Prune:* Training and clean-up only. While dormant.

Amorpha   *Indigo bush*

Habit: Open, arching. *Train:* Specimen, copse. *Prune:* Mild: While dormant head back to firm wood. Cold: Cut back as new growth starts, to remove frozen wood. Will stump sprout if cut to ground.

Arbutus unedo   *Strawberry-tree*

Habit: Compact, round-headed. *Train:* Specimen. *Prune:* Prune very lightly for shaping only. Can be headed to control height. Mild: As growth starts in spring.

Aronia   *Chokeberry*

Habit: Thin, spreading. *Train:* Natural, wild planting. *Prune:* Head back lightly to encourage lateral growth. Do not remove suckers unless too far from plant. Mild or cold: As soon as the berries have dropped.

Aster fruticosus   *Shrub aster*

Habit: Compact, woody shrub. *Train:* Shrub border, low informal hedge. *Prune:* Cut back to unflowered laterals. Remove weak and spindly branches. Mild: After flowering.

Aucuba japonica   *Gold-dust tree*

Habit: Compact, bushy. *Train:* Specimen, tub plant. *Prune:* After frost, remove dead or damaged wood. May be cut severely if necessary for renewing an old plant. Tip pinching will cause laterals to form. Mild: Late spring.

Azalea

See Chapter Five.

Azara

Habit: Open, arching. *Train:* Specimen, one of the best wall or espalier shrubs. *Prune:* Shaping only. Will stand severe pruning. Mild: Any time.

Bamboo   *(Bambusa, Phyllostachys, others)*

Habit: Tight clumps. *Train:* Specimen, hedge, screen. Usually grown naturally. *Prune:* May be thinned to good advantage to permit new canes to develop. Do not leave stubs. Always cut at or just below ground. Dwarf varieties stand shearing well. Mild: Spring. Old thick stands can be cut back to the ground and will quickly develop fresh new clumps.

Bauhinia Galpinii

Habit: Half-climbing shrub. *Train:* Specimen, wall plant. *Prune:* Training only. Mild: Spring.

Bauhinia variegata   *Mountain ebony, orchid-tree*

Habit: Loose, open. *Train:* Specimen, standard. *Prune:* Clean-up pruning only. Seed pods may be removed to advantage. Mild: After flowering.

Benzoin   *Spice bush*

Habit: Bushy, arching. *Train:* Specimen. *Prune:* Thin lightly and train. Mild or cold: While dormant.

Berberis *Barberry*

Habit: Dense, bushy. *Train:* Formal or informal shrub border or hedge, mass planting. *Prune:* Control pruning only. Every few years cut back and thin for wood renewal. Mild or cold: Spring after berry show is past.

Bouvardia

Habit: Spreading, rapid. *Train:* Specimen, border, low trellis. *Prune:* Bloom all year if given at least one severe pruning a year. Two prunings a year may be given in frost-free areas. Constantly renew the wood by thinning and heading. Mild: Main pruning after a heavy bloom.

Brachysema acuminatum

Habit: Willowy. *Train:* Specimen. *Prune:* Thin and head back to avoid staking and tying. Will break out if severely pruned. Mild: Spring.

Brunfelsia *Yesterday-today-and-tomorrow*

Habit: Compact. *Train:* Specimen. *Prune:* Training only, remove spent flowering wood. Mild: Spring.

Buddleja *Summer lilac, butterfly-bush*

Habit: Open, spreading, vigorous. *Prune:* Cut back hard. Remove a few of the oldest stumps each year. Thin out new growth. Will stand cutting to ground. Mild: After flowering. Frosty: Spring. Cold: Fall, cover roots.

Buxus *Box, boxwood*

Habit: Neat, compact, round headed. *Train:* Specimen, tub plant, hedge, topiary. *Prune:* Shaping only to keep compact. Stands frequent clipping. Breaks well from old wood. Mild or cold: Any time from spring to early fall.

Calliandra *Trinidad flame-bush*

Habit: Open, feathery. *Train:* Specimen. *Prune:* Tip pinch lightly to promote bushiness and prevent tendency to legginess. Mild: Spring and summer.

Callicarpa *Beauty-berry*

Habit: Bushy, arching. *Train:* Natural. *Prune:* Cut back hard to produce new fruiting wood. In cold areas will freeze to ground. Remove entire top and new growth will soon develop. If new growth is too strong it can be tip pinched. Mild: After berries are gone. Cold: Spring.

Callistemon *Bottle-brush*

Habit: Tall, slender, semi-weeping. *Train:* Specimen, wall shrub. *Prune:* Needs very little pruning. Tip pinching while young will promote bushiness and prevent legginess. Careful pruning will increase bloom. Do *not* cut below leaves as they do not break well from old wood. Mild: Fall.

Calycanthus floridus *Carolina allspice, sweet-shrub, strawberry-shrub*

Habit: Open, spreading. *Train:* Natural. *Prune:* Light shaping and thinning. Remove old shoots back to short spurs for wood renewal. Mild or cold: After flowering.

Camellia

Habit: Compact. *Train:* Specimen, tub plant, hedge, espalier. *Prune:* Head back lightly for compactness. Willowy growing varieties will require annual pruning. Old plants may be severely cut back without damage. Remove spent flowers and prevent seed from forming. Mild: During or immediately after flowering.

Caragana *Siberian pea*

Habit: Open, spreading. *Train:* Specimen, hedge. *Prune:* Head back lightly for compactness while young. Will stand severe pruning. Mild or cold: After flowering.

Carissa *Natal-plum*

Habit: Irregular. *Train:* Specimen, tub plant, hedge. *Prune:* Needs early training as branches are prostrate at first. Keep heading new growth until a strong framework is established. Mild: Late spring.

Caryopteris *Bluebeard*

Habit: Bushy. *Train:* Specimen. *Prune:* Cut back hard to encourage new growth. Will freeze to ground in cold areas. If frozen, remove entire top. New growth will spring up. Mild: Fall. Cold: Spring.

Cassia *Golden wonder*

Habit: Large, spreading shrub. *Train:* Specimen. *Prune:* Thin out while small to develop good framework. After flowering cut all new growth back to short spurs. This removes seed pods and forces new blooming wood to develop. Mild: After flowering.

Ceanothus *California wild lilac*

Habit: Various. *Train:* Specimen, ground covers, natural. *Prune:* Any shaping or pruning should be done immediately after flowering. Dwarf and prostrate forms will stand fairly severe pruning. Shrubby and tree types should be lightly pruned. The new hybrids should be tipped to promote bushiness. Top branches can be removed directly above a lateral. Some species stump sprout freely under favorable cultural conditions, but this should only be encouraged under extreme circumstances, and on a trial basis.

Ceratostigma *Plumbago*

Habit: Trailing. *Train:* Natural. *Prune:* Head back one-third and thin for early bloom. Cut to ground for later bloom. Mild: While dormant.

Cestrum

Habit: Tall, arching. *Train:* Specimen, wall shrub, pillar. *Prune:* Cut back old shoots to unflowered laterals. Each spring remove some of the oldest canes. When frosted, wait until new growth starts before cutting back. Mild: Spring.

Chaenomeles (Cydonia) *Flowering quince, Japanese quince*

Habit: Congested, spreading. *Train:* Specimen, hedge, wall plant. *Prune:* One spring flowering shrub that is pruned in winter because flowers are borne on wood that is two or more years old. Thin out weak branches and suckers. Prevent tangling and crossing. Cut back one-year wood at least a third. Mild or cold: While dormant.

Chamaelaucium *Geraldton wax flower*

Habit: Graceful, open. *Train:* Natural. *Prune:* Use flowers freely then cut back hard. Always leave some spurs of the current growth. Mild: After flowering.

Chimonanthus *Winter sweet*

Habit: Compact. *Train:* Specimen. *Prune:* Thin and head slightly. Mild or cold: After flowering.

Chionanthus virginica *White fringe-tree*

Habit: Neat, compact. *Train:* Natural. *Prune:* Thin only, as flowers are borne near the tips of year-old branches followed by fruit on pistillate forms.

Choisya ternata *Mexican-orange*

Habit: Thick, compact, leafy. *Train:* Specimen, group, hedge. *Prune:* Trim lightly and thin out to permit light to reach center of plant. When plants become shabby after a few years, cut back hard and thin freely. Will stand any amount of pruning and will stump sprout. Mild: After flowering.

Chorizema *Flowering oak*

Habit: Trailing. *Train:* Ground cover, hanging over wall, low trellis. *Prune:* Cut back hard to remove seed pods and encourage new growth. Remove weak and dead shoots. Mild: After flowering.

Cistus *Rock-rose*

Habit: Compact, twiggy, some varieties trailing. *Train:* Natural, ground cover, or mass. *Prune:* Needs no prun-

ing. May be headed back to laterals to control size. Do not cut into leafless old stems. Varieties that hold dead flower stems should be sheared for neatness.

Clethra alnifolia *Summer sweet, sweet pepperbush*

Habit: Bushy. *Train:* Natural. *Prune:* Training only.

Clethra arborea *Lily-of-the-valley tree*

Habit: Fastigiate. *Train:* Specimen. *Prune:* No pruning required. Spent flowers may be removed if desired.

Clianthus puniceus *Parrots-bill*

Habit: Half-trailing. *Train:* Wall shrub, trellis plant. *Prune:* Shape and train. Remove weak laterals. Clip out spent flower trusses. Mild: Late spring.

Coleonema (also see Diosma) *Pink breath of heaven*

Habit: Compact, bushy. *Train:* Natural. *Prune:* Shear back to prevent flopping. Has weak stem and root structure. Will stand severe pruning. Mild: After flowering.

Comarostaphylis *Summer holly*

Habit: Compact. *Train:* Specimen. *Prune:* Training or corrective only.

Coprosma *Mirror plant*

Habit: Vigorous, spreading. *Train:* ground cover, specimen, wall plant, hedge. *Prune:* Shape, head too-vigorous shoots any time. Stands frequent shearing and any amount of pruning. Mild: Fall or spring.

Cornus (Twig types) *Dogwood*

Habit: Clump, stiff upright, twiggy. *Train:* Natural, copse. *Prune:* Cut all growth back to short spurs to produce as many young, highly colored shoots as possible. Mild or cold: Spring.

Coronilla

Habit: Sprawling, weak. *Train:* Specimen, wall plant. *Prune:* Needs shaping to prevent sprawling. Stands light shearing. Do not prune back to old wood. Encourage basal growth for renewal of old stems. Mild: After flowering.

Correa *Australian fuchsia*

Habit: Spreading, leggy. *Train:* Specimen, ground cover, low trellis. *Prune:* Head lightly to promote bushiness. Inclined to lose lower leaves and become leggy. Do not cut below leaves or laterals as they break poorly from old wood. Mild: After flowering.

Cotoneaster

Habit: Various. *Train:* Various according to species as: Specimen, ground cover, standard, hedge, wall plant. *Prune:* Pruning usually desirable for control and neatness. Use berries freely, cutting back to unflowered laterals. Remove only old shoots that have berried. If strong laterals are not present, remove entire branch to trunk or ground level. Dwarf and creeping species need only shaping. However, all of them stand heavy pruning well and will break from old wood if severe measures are called for. Heavy pruning means the loss of one crop of berries. Mild or cold: As soon as berries fall.

Crotalaria agatiflora   *Canary-bird flower*

Habit: Tall, arching. *Train:* Specimen. *Prune:* Do not tip new growth. Cut back hard after blooming. If frozen to ground, will soon recover.

Cytisus   *Broom, Sweet-broom*

Habit: Spreading. *Train:* Specimen, standard, formal or informal hedge, wall plant. *Prune:* Cut back the shoots that have flowered to remove the heavy crop of seed pods. Try to leave some of the young wood. Does not break well from old wood. Mild: after flowering.

Daboecia cantabrica   *St. Daboeck's heath, Irish bell heather*

Habit: Neat, thick, compact. *Train:* Ground cover, mass planting. *Prune:* Shear back lightly to prevent seeding and for neatness. Mild: After flowering.

Daphne   *Garland flower*

Habit: Compact. *Train:* Specimen. *Prune:* Pruning rarely necessary. Mild: During or immediately after flowering.

Deutzia

Habit: Spreading, arching. *Train:* Specimen or mass planting. *Prune:* Head back to strong laterals. Remove weak growths entirely. Cut out a few of the oldest branches each year. Mild or cold: After flowering.

Diosma (Coleonema)   *Breath of heaven*

Habit: Compact. *Train:* Specimen, mass planting, formal or informal hedge. *Prune:* Can be sheared for compactness. May be cut back hard. Mild: After main crop of bloom.

Duranta   *Brazil sky-flower*

Habit: Arching. *Train:* Specimen. *Prune:* Remove branches that have produced berries back to the ground or to strong unflowered laterals. Do not tip prune, as new growth bunches just below cuts. Mild: Spring.

Echium fastuosum   *Pride of Madeira*

Habit: Round-topped clump. *Train:* Natural, singly or mass planting. *Prune:* Remove flower spikes as soon as flowers have faded.

Elaeagnus

Habit: Bushy, spreading. *Train:* Specimen, wall shrub, hedge. *Prune:* Shaping only but will stand heavy pruning.

Erica   *Heather*

Habit: Compact. *Train:* Specimen, mass planting. *Prune:* Remove entire flower spike back to unflowered shoots. Eliminate old "knuckles" where possible. Will break from fairly old wood. Dwarf European heathers should be sheared back. Mild: After flowering.

Escallonia

Habit: Bushy, vigorous, twiggy. *Train:* Specimen, mass, formal or informal hedge, wall plant. *Prune:* Cut back hard and thin severely. Head laterals to short spurs. Remove one-third of the old woody growth each year. Keep an equal number of the strongest suckers for wood renewal. If size of flower is unimportant and room is available, this heavy pruning could be performed every other or third year. Will stand any amount of pruning or shearing and will stump sprout. The newer, small-leaved hybrids may be pruned every third year except for light cleanup. Mild: After flowering or winter.

Eugenia

Habit: Compact, columnar, weak stems. *Train:* Specimen, tub plants, hedge. *Prune:* Allow only one leader or trunk as crotches are very weak. Lighten branches to prevent breakage. May be topped to control height. Will stand any amount of clipping or pruning. Mild: Spring after danger of frost is past.

Euonymus

Habit: Irregular, half-climbing. *Train:* Specimen, tub plant, wall plant, hedge. *Prune:* Shape only. Head back ungainly shoots. Occasionally, remove some of the congested old wood from interior of plant. Remove all green-leaved shoots from variegated forms immediately or they will quickly ruin the plants. Will stand very severe pruning. Mild: Any time. Cold: Spring.

Euphorbia   *Poinsettia*

Habit: Open, spreading. *Train:* Espalier. *Prune:* Cut back all one-year wood to short spurs after danger of frost is past. Do not leave more than two buds on each spur. After the plant is a few years old, some of its old "knuckles" should be removed annually. Entire head can be removed if necessary without losing plant. Mild: After flowering.

Euryops   *South African daisy-bush, Silver and gold bush*

Habit: Dwarf, compact. *Train:* Natural. *Prune:* No pruning necessary. Remove spent flowers if desired.

Exochorda   *Pearl-bush*

Habit: Open, spreading. *Train:* Specimen. *Prune:* Needs little pruning. Shape and thin lightly. Wood renewal is unnecessary. Mild or cold: After flowering.

Fatsia (Aralia)

Habit: Clump. *Train:* Specimen, tub plant. *Prune:* Remove spent fruit clusters. Old canes cut back will generally stump sprout. Mild: Spring.

Feijoa   *Guava*

Habit: Compact. *Train:* Specimen, tub plant. *Prune:* Corrective pruning only. May be severely pruned if desired. If badly frosted and defoliated will generally break freely from old wood. Do not cut back too soon. Wait until new buds are well advanced. Mild: Late spring.

Ficus   *Rubber plant*

Habit: Compact, round-headed. *Train:* Specimen, tub plant. *Prune:* Cut as little as possible. Bleeding is not fatal but unsightly.

Forsythia   *Golden-bells*

Habit: Tall, pendulous. *Train:* Specimen, natural. *Prune:* Control pruning and training. Do not remove or head back the beautiful pendulous branches until they become old and woody. Cut old wood back to the ground and thin out weak, crowded growths. Mild or cold: After flowering.

Fremontia

Habit: Spreading. *Train:* Specimen, wall or espalier. *Prune:* Remove weak and pendulous shoots. Head back to laterals to control size and shape. May be pruned severely. Mild: After flowering.

Fuchsia   *Jewel flower*

Habit: Vigorous, half-climbers, soft, leafy. *Train:* Natural, mass, specimen, hedge, pillar, standard, vine, wall shrub, espalier. *Prune:* Prune heavily to short, sturdy spurs. Thin freely. Must be followed by tip pinching throughout summer growing season. Mild: Winter. Cool: Late spring after frosts.

Shrub fuchsia   *Tree fuchsia*

Gardenia

Habit: Bushy. *Train:* Specimen, tub plant. *Prune:* No pruning required as a rule. Prevent legginess by heading top shoots that grow too rapidly. Some thinning may be necessary.

Gaultheria

Habit: Bushy or creeping. *Train:* Specimen, ground cover, natural shade garden. *Prune:* Pruning rarely necessary except to remove any sign of die-back, which is troublesome in some areas. Spent berrying shoots may be clipped out to advantage.

Genista

(See Cytisus)

Genista monosperma   *Bridal veil shrub*

Habit: Thin upright with weeping branches. *Train:* Specimen. Weak stem and roots. Needs careful staking until well established. *Prune:* No pruning is essential, but the plant will stand considerable cutting if carefully done. Mild: After flowering.

Grevillea Thelemanniana   *Jewel flower*

Habit: Soft, compact. *Train:* Specimen, mass. *Prune:* Light control only. Resents disturbance of any kind.

Hakea

Habit: Compact heads, leggy stems. *Train:* Specimen, mass. Spiny species make good informal barrier hedges. *Prune:* Tip lightly while young to promote bushiness. Never shear, as recovery is slow and cut stems look stubby. Does not break well from old wood.

Hamamelis   *Witch-hazel*

Habit: Neat. *Train:* Specimen, wild planting. *Prune:* Training only.

Hebe (Veronica)

Habit: Compact, dome-shaped. *Train:* Specimen, mass planting, formal or informal hedge. *Prune:* Remove spent blooms, and shape lightly. May be held to any desired size indefinitely. Every few years, or when considered necessary, cut back hard and thin freely. Remove old, cracked and scale-infested wood to ground level. Will break from old wood and will stand any amount of clipping or pruning. Mild: After the main crop of bloom, which varies with species.

Heliotropium   *Heliotrope*

Habit: Weak, half-trailing. *Train:* Bedding, tub plant, low trellis, ground cover. *Prune:* Remove spent flowers and weak shoots. Cut back for bushiness. Mild: Spring after danger of frost.

Heteromeles (Photinia)   *Toyon, California Holly, Christmas-berry*

Habit: Compact, round-headed. *Train:* Specimen, mass, wild planting. *Prune:* Shaping and cleanup. Will stand heavy pruning and heading if absolutely necessary. Mild or cold: Spring.

Hibiscus   *Perennial types*

Cut to ground in fall.

Hibiscus Rosa-sinensis   *Chinese hibiscus*

Habit: Open, symmetrical. *Prune:* Head back to produce flowering wood. As much as a third of the old wood can be removed back to strong laterals. Mild: Spring.

Hibiscus syriacus   *Rose-of-Sharon*

Habit: Strong, upright. *Train:* Specimen. There are two methods of training widely used. One way, if size of flower is unimportant, is to allow plant to make a large shrub by light pruning and thinning. Other method, which gets the best from this shrub, is to prune severely, cutting back all of the year-old wood to two or three buds or eyes. Mild: Fall. Cold: Spring.

Hydrangea macrophylla (Opuloides, Hortensis) *Common evergreen hydrangea*

Habit: Clump, strong upright. *Train:* Specimen, bedding, mass. *Prune:* As flowers fade, remove the stem back to strong unflowered laterals or well developed buds. Do not cut back unflowered shoots. Buds set in summer, bloom seven or eight months later. Old plantings may be cut to the ground when they become woody or stubby. They will respond with increased vigor, but will not bloom for some time. Mild: After flowering.

Hydrangea arborescens   *Hills-of-snow*

Hydrangea paniculata grandiflora   *Peegee hydrangea*

Habit: Deciduous, woody shrubs. *Train:* Specimen, standards, mass. *Prune:* May be allowed to develop naturally, which results in numerous, but small, flowers. It is best to remove some of the old branches entirely and head back the year-old wood to short two- to four-bud spurs. Thin the new growth that results, retaining enough of the strongest shoots for renewal the following year. Standards, once the heads are formed, should be spur-pruned each winter, leaving only two buds on well-placed branches. This severe pruning constantly renews the plants and keeps them in the peak of condition and produces enormous heads of flowers. Mild or cold: While dormant. Remove spent flowers after bloom has passed.

Hypericum   *St. Johnswort*

Habit: Compact, twiggy. *Train:* Specimen, bedding, wall shrub, hedge. *Prune:* Thin out all thin and weak growth and suckers. Head back year-old shoots to short spurs. Can stand heavy shearing or pruning. *H. Calycinum,* used as a ground cover, should be sheared or mowed to the ground when it becomes woody and unsightly. Mild or cold: Spring, just as new growth starts.

Ilex *Holly*

Habit: Dense, even, pyramidal or round-topped. *Train:* Specimen, hedge. Train to single dominant trunk. *Prune:* Remove suckers. Head lightly whenever necessary. Will stand heavy pruning and shaping. Mild or cold: Any time, but use for Christmas decorations will generally suffice.

Iochroma

Habit: Arching. *Train:* Specimen, wall shrub. *Prune:* Prune severely, removing old shoots to ground. Encourage sucker growth, as flowers are borne on strong new wood.

Itea ilicifolia *Holly-leaf sweet spire*

Habit: Tall, slender. *Train:* Specimen. *Prune:* Shaping only.

Itea virginica *Virginia-willow, sweet spire*

Habit: Open. *Train:* Natural. *Prune:* Head back lightly and thin out old wood. Mild: Fall. Cold: Spring.

Kalmia *Mountain-laurel*

Habit: Compact. *Train:* Specimen, mass. *Prune:* Remove spent flowers. Heading back old plants will make them compact and promote healthy new growth. Will stand severe cutting. Mild or cold: After flowering.

Kerria (Corchorus)

Habit: Half-climbing, spreading. *Train:* Specimen, copse, wall plant, hedge. *Prune:* Remove old canes to encourage new growth. Lightly head year-old canes and thin if necessary. Remove suckers that are too far from the plant to be of use. Mild or cold: After flowering.

Kolkwitzia *Beauty-bush*

Habit: Compact, twiggy. *Train:* Specimen only, do not hedge. *Prune:* Prune lightly if at all. Flowers are best when plant of some age and size. Wood renewal not necessary. Heavy pruning means the loss of at least one season's flowering.

Lantana

Habit: Trailing. *Train:* Specimen, bedding, ground cover, wall plant, trellis plant. *Prune:* Cut back hard and remove long, weak shoots. Will break from old wood and will stump sprout. Mild: Spring.

Laurus nobilis *Laurel*

Habit: Bushy, round-headed, shapely. *Train:* Specimen, standard, tub plant. *Prune:* Stands shaping into any form. May be heavily pruned. Mild: Prune in spring, clip during summer.

Lavandula *Lavender*

Habit: Compact. *Train:* Specimen, low hedge or edging. *Prune:* Head back to strong unflowered laterals. Thin out weak growth. Mild: After flowering.

Leonotis *Lions-ear*

Habit: Rank, soft, sprawling. *Train:* Specimen, wall shrub, screen plant. *Prune:* Remove weak growth and sprawling stems. After first blooms are over, start a continuous pruning program. Remove each spent bloom well back to the strong basal laterals. The entire plant will be renewed during the flowering season. May be cut to the ground in late spring if desired or if frosted.

Leptospermum *Australian tea-tree*

Habit: Spreading and sprawling. *Train:* Specimen, formal or informal hedge, mass, windbreak. Should be shaped and trained while young. Stems and roots are weak and plants will grow horizontally unless staked or heavily pruned. *Prune:* Cut back to laterals and be sure to leave some foliage, as it will not break from old wood. Mild: Shaping may be done any time. The small-leaved types, including the new hybrids, are neat and compact and need practically no pruning.

Leucothoe

Habit: Spreading. *Train:* Natural, wild planting. *Prune:* Remove spent flowering shoots back to strong laterals. Remove some of the oldest canes each year to make room for vigorous new shoots from the roots. Mild or cold: After flowering.

Ligustrum *Privet*

Habit: Bushy, twiggy. *Train:* Specimen, hedge. *Prune:* Will stand any amount of pruning or shearing. If not pruned, makes a graceful shrub that blooms freely and sets clusters of black berries. Mild: Any time. Cold: Spring.

Lippia citriodora *Lemon-verbena*

Habit: Spreading, irregular. *Train:* Specimen. *Prune:* Needs severe heading to keep it within bounds. Thin out weak growth. Mild: While dormant.

Lonicera (shrub types) *Berried honeysuckle*

Habit: Neat, twiggy. *Train:* Specimen, mass, hedge. *Prune:* Thin out only when needed which may be every four or five years. *L. nitida* stands shearing and shaping. Once much used for topiary work. When grown naturally, old shoots that become congested and untidy should be removed.

Mahonia   *Oregon-grape*

Habit: Compact, spreading clump. *Train:* Specimen, copse, informal hedge. *Prune:* No pruning necessary. Old canes may be removed when they become leggy. They will usually stump sprout.

Melaleuca   *Bottle-brush*

Habit: Straggly, leggy. *Train:* Specimen, mass. *Prune:* Head lightly while young to promote bushiness. Does not break well from old wood. Mild: Spring.

Michelia   *Banana-shrub*

Habit: Compact, bushy. *Train:* Specimen. *Prune:* No pruning necessary but may be shaped if desired.

Myrsine africana   *African boxwood*

Habit: Dense, compact, leafy. *Train:* Specimen, formal or informal hedge. *Prune:* No pruning necessary, but will stand any amount of pruning and shaping. Will grow from roots if top is destroyed.

Myrtus   *Myrtle*

Habit: Dense, compact. *Train:* Specimen, mass, hedge. *Prune:* May be left unpruned, but stands pruning well. May be clipped frequently for formal use. Mild: Spring.

Nandina   *Heavenly bamboo*

Habit: Clump. *Train:* Specimen, mass. *Prune:* Requires no pruning until it becomes leggy. Then remove a few of the oldest canes. Encourage all sucker and basal growths. Mild: As growth starts in spring.

Nerium   *Oleander*

Habit: Tall, arching. *Train:* Specimen, standard, informal hedge. May be trained as shrub or tree. *Prune:* Remove old wood that has flowered. Head lightly where size must be controlled. Closer pruning will prevent flower heads from weighting down the branches. Suckers badly. Suckers may be left on shrub type, but should be dug out from around tree types. Mild: Spring.

Osmanthus   *Sweet olive*

Habit: Compact. *Train:* Specimen. *Prune:* No pruning necessary. Shape while young.

Philadelphus   *Mock-orange*

Habit: Stout, arching. *Train:* Specimen, mass, wall shrub. *Prune:* Remove spent flowers by cutting canes about one-half or to strong unflowered laterals. Old woody branches should be cut off at ground level. Allow strong suckers to develop, but remove weak and overcrowded ones. Mild or cold: After flowering.

Photinia

Habit: Round-headed. *Train:* Specimen. *Prune:* Training only.

Physocarpus   *Ninebark*

Habit: Clump forming, open. *Train:* Specimen, mass, natural. *Prune:* Prune like *Spiraea* (which see). Remove spent flowering wood during dormant season because seed pods are attractive after bloom. Keep renewing wood from base by cutting a few old shoots back to the ground yearly.

Pieris   *Andromeda*

Habit: Compact. *Train:* Specimen. *Prune:* Little pruning necessary. May be cut back hard if required.

Pimelea   *Rice-flower*

Habit: Compact, cone-shaped. *Train:* Specimen. *Prune:* Head lightly after flowering, being careful to leave some foliage. Does not respond well to severe pruning.

Pittosporum

Habit: Compact, regular. *Train:* As shrub or small tree, tub plant, formal or informal hedge, windbreak. *Prune:* Training and control. Will stand very severe pruning. Tree types should be trained to single trunks, as large crotches are weak. Over-extended branches on all types should be headed back. Mild: Any time. Cold: Spring.

Polygala

Habit: Bushy, dome shaped. *Train:* Specimen, mass, bedding. *Prune:* Head lightly to prevent legginess. Will stand rather severe pruning. Mild: After heaviest bloom in late summer.

Prunus   *Evergreen types*
Prunus caroliniana   *Carolina cherry, Wild-orange*
Prunus ilicifolia   *Holly-leaf cherry*
Prunus Laurocerasus   *Cherry-laurel*
Prunus lusitanica   *Portugal-laurel*
Prunus Lyonii   *Catalina cherry*

Habit: Compact, bushy. *Train:* Specimen, formal or informal hedge. *Prune:* Train and shape. Will stand heavy pruning and topping. Mild: Any time.

Punica *Dwarf pomegranate*

Habit: Compact, twiggy. *Train:* Specimen, hedge, tub plant. *Prune:* All year-old wood should be headed back sharply to encourage the new shoots upon which the flowers are borne. Thin out all weak growth and any of the center branches that have become old and stubby. Mild or cool: Winter.

Pyracantha *Firethorn*

Habit: Bushy or sprawling. *Train:* Specimen, ground cover, hedge, wall plant. *Prune:* Pruning is not essential but is desirable for control and neatness. Tip pinching throughout the year is a good practice. When cutting berries, remove the entire branch back to unflowered laterals or to ground level. New growth is inclined to bunch just below the cut of a headed branch. Maximum crops of berries are produced by plants that have all of the wood which bore previously removed as soon as the berries have dropped. Will stand very heavy pruning, but if year-old branches are removed, one crop of berries will be lost. Mild: During and just after berrying.

Raphiolepis

Habit: Compact. *Train:* Specimen, tub plant, ground cover, wall plant. *Prune:* Stands pruning and training well, but very little is necessary. "Runaway" branches should be removed at their source.

Rhamnus Alaternus

Habit: Upright, bushy. *Train:* Specimen, hedge. *Prune:* May be pruned or sheared as heavily as desired. Will break from wood of any age. Mild: Fall.

Rhamnus californica *Coffee-berry*

Habit: Compact, dome shaped. *Train:* Specimen. *Prune:* Very little pruning needed; however, will stump sprout if cut back. Mild: fall.

Rhododendron

See Chapter Five.

Rhodotypos kerrioides *Jetbead*

Habit: Compact, twiggy. *Train:* Specimen. *Prune:* After berries have dropped, lightly thin out oldest wood. Do not tip, as spring flowers are terminal on new wood. Encourage a few sturdy sucker growths for renewal.

Rhus *Sumac, Smoke-tree*

Habit: Clump forming. *Train:* Specimen, copse. *Prune:* May be allowed to grow naturally. Some prefer to cut entire plant off at the ground early in spring to develop all new, highly colored wood.

Ribes *Gooseberry, Flowering currant*

Habit: Bushy. *Train:* Specimen, natural. *Prune:* Remove weak shoots. Renew old plants by cutting back a few of the oldest stems to ground annually. Do not head new shoots at this time, or flowers will be lost. Mild or cold: Early fall.

Romneya *Matilija-poppy*

Habit: Wide-spreading clump. *Train:* Specimen. *Prune:* Early each fall cut back to short spurs. In cold areas give winter protection by covering with heavy mulch. In mild climates new growth starts immediately.

Roses

See Chapter Six.

Rosmarinus *Rosemary*

Habit: Bushy. *Train:* Specimen, tub plant, low hedge. *Prune:* Light summer pruning to remove spent flowers and control size and shape.

Salvia (shrubby species) *Sage*

Habit: Sprawling, bushy. *Train:* Specimen, mass. *Prune:* Thin freely removing all old wood. Neglected plants may be cut off at the ground and will rapidly regrow. Mild: Spring.

Sarcococca

Habit: Neat, compact clump. *Train:* Specimen, informal low hedge. *Prune:* May be shaped, but needs no pruning. If cut back to the ground, will sprout from roots.

Skimmia

Habit: Bushy, dome-shaped. *Train:* Natural. *Prune:* No pruning required.

Spartium *Spanish broom*

Habit: Leggy, sprawling. *Train:* Specimen, mass. *Prune:* Head back heavily each year for compactness. Mild: Late summer or fall.

Sphaeralcea *Mexican-mallow*

Habit: Rapid, soft, bushy. *Train:* Specimen, informal hedge or windbreak. *Prune:* Remove spent wood, old canes. Head back balance to firm wood or unflowered laterals. Mild: Fall.

Spiraea *Bridal wreath*

Habit: Open, arching, clump forming. *Train:* Specimen, mass. *Prune:* As soon as blooming season is over, remove all wood that flowered back to strong buds or young shoots. Strong new wood from the base is lightly headed to encourage laterals. A few old shoots should be removed entirely each year. Well pruned spiraea should never need tying or staking. The summer-flowering spiraeas, Bumalda and Douglasii, should be thinned and headed to produce new wood while dormant.

Staphylea   *Bladder-nut*

Habit: Upright shrub or small tree. *Train:* Specimen. *Prune:* Training and shaping.

Stephanandra

Habit: Low, compact. *Train:* Natural. *Prune:* Thin out wood that flowered, cutting back to strong laterals or to base. Allow suckers to grow freely. Mild or cold: While dormant.

Symphoricarpos   *Snowberry*

Habit: Loose, spreading. *Train:* Natural, copse, wild planting. *Prune:* Remove old scrubby canes. Encourage sucker growth. Thick, tangled beds may be cut back to the ground every few years. Mild or cold: While dormant.

Syringa   *Lilac*

Habit: Strong, woody, round-topped. *Train:* Specimen. *Prune:* Cutting of flowers fulfills some of the pruning requirements, but all spent flowers should be removed immediately. If plants are grafted, all suckers should be religiously cut out. Thinning the wood in winter will result in fewer, but much finer, flower clusters. Old plants may be renewed, and at the same time decreased in size, by removing one-third of the old branches each year, until all have been removed. The new growth resulting from the first heading will flower when the last third is removed; hence, the plants are never entirely without bloom.

Tamarix

Habit: Sprawling, arching. *Train:* Specimen, ground cover, copse, informal hedge. *Prune:* The spring-flowering species bloom on last year's wood and should be pruned immediately after flowering. The late-flowering species bloom in panicles on the current growth, so are heavily headed while dormant to produce quantities of new shoots. They all need considerable control pruning and may be cut to the ground when necessary.

Tetrapanax (Aralia)   *Rice-paper plant*

Habit: Tall, leggy. *Train:* Specimen, tub plant. *Prune:* Will rarely make laterals unless headed. Remove entire head to desired height. It will usually break freely just below the cut, or from the base. A bushy plant will permit occasional removal of overgrown canes. Mild: Late spring.

Teucrium

Habit: Sprawling, irregular. *Train:* Specimen, mass, hedge. *Prune:* Head back for shape. Stands pruning and clipping well. Will root-sprout if old plants are cut back. Mild: Fall.

Tibouchina (Pleroma, Lasiandra)   *Princess-flower, Glory-bush*

Habit: Stiffly erect. *Train:* Specimen, wall plant. *Prune:* Remove all thin weak growths. Head back all branches to strong buds. If frosted, wait until new growth starts before cutting back to sound wood. Will stem- or stump-sprout if entire head is killed or removed. If size must be controlled, can be spur-pruned to one-joint spurs. Mild: Late spring.

Vaccinium   *Huckleberry*

Habit: Bushy, clump forming. *Train:* Natural. *Prune:* Shaping only. Stands pruning well and will stump-sprout. Mild or cold: Fall.

Veronica

See *Hebe*

Viburnum

Habit: Various. *Train:* Specimen, mass.

Viburnum Opulus sterile   *Snowball, Guelder-rose*

Viburnum tomentosum plenum   *Japanese snowball*

The two deciduous species listed above are woody shrubs that should be lightly cut back after flowering. Remove all spent flowering wood back to strong buds or unflowered laterals. The other species and varieties need very little pruning, except to control size and maintain a bushy and healthy condition. However, they will all recover quickly from severe pruning.

Weigela (Diervilla)

Habit: Tall, arching. *Train:* Specimen, mass. *Prune:* Prune out all wood that flowered back to strong, unflowered laterals or back to ground level. Leave only one or two laterals per stem. Cut out some of the oldest stumps. Thin sucker growth to a few of the best. Tip lightly in midsummer if growth is too rank. Mild or cold: After flowering.

Xylosma senticosa

Habit: Spreading. *Train:* Specimen. *Prune:* Needs no pruning.

CHAPTER 5. Rhododendrons and Azaleas

The genus rhododendron, which also includes all of the azaleas, is rapidly becoming of great interest and importance to ornamental horticulture. The formation of the American Rhododendron Society, with headquarters in Oregon, greatly stimulated interest in this magnificent shrub. Many new hybrids have been imported and propagated and are now available to the gardening public. The catalogs, which until recently listed but four or five varieties, now list from 25 to 50 varieties, in a wide range of color and of many different growth habits. The hundreds of species introduced from seed sent in by the famous plant collectors, such as Forrest, Kingdon-Ward, and Rock, have been matured and evaluated, and the best species have been selected, propagated and disseminated. Many of these are hardier than the hybrids and they will further extend the range of usefulness of the genus.

For a great many years, the obtainable varieties always included Pink Pearl, Alice, and Cynthia. Pink Pearl was the great favorite and literally thousands of them have been planted wherever they were hardy. It, like the other two mentioned, is a vigorously growing hybrid and under favorable conditions is capable of becoming a small tree. But many a treasured plant of Pink Pearl, planted under a window where it could be carefully watched, has become a gawky, leggy, sparse-foliaged giant, bearing its lovely flowers too high to be enjoyed. This condition is entirely unnecessary and proper pruning would have prevented it. What? Prune a rhododendron? Of course. Why not?

For some reason, it has been an established custom never to prune a rhododendron. The gardener who slashes everything else in sight, pauses in awe when he reaches the "king of shrubs." Many garden club lecturers still state with conviction that shears must never touch this royal plant, even going so far as to say that the flowers should never be cut for indoor decoration. This is all very foolish and pointless. There is no reason why these lovely flowers should not be enjoyed in the home. They make fabulous arrangements and last as well as or better than most cut blooms. Three or five trusses are enough to make a good show, and even a single plant can provide them easily without spoiling the garden effect. If selected properly, they help to keep the plant within bounds and to preserve the tight and compact habit that helps give them their air of distinction.

When to Prune

Rhododendrons are in their most dormant condition at blooming time; so the removal of flowers comes at the proper time for the good of the plant. The balance of the pruning should be done immediately after the last flowers have faded, for that is when the new cycle of growth commences and is rapidly carried forward. A rhododendron branch, headed back immediately after blooming, is capable of producing new shoots from dormant buds that will bloom the following spring. Generally, however, under average garden conditions, the pruned branches will set only leaf buds the first year and produce heavy trusses the second season. For this reason, it is far better to head back not more than one-third of the branches each year to insure a good show of bloom each spring.

Removal of Blooms

Whether or not you wish to remove or head back any branches of your rhododendron, there is one form of pruning that must always be practiced if you wish to have good bloom each year. Remove every one of the spent trusses as soon as the flowers have faded. The fleshy, cone-shaped spur that supports the truss is usually soft and may be removed with the thumb nail or a light pair of shears. The important thing is to remove these without damaging the circle of buds that are just starting into growth at the base of the flower stem. These buds make the shoots which will carry the flowers the following year.

If they are damaged or removed with the spent flower, there will be no bloom on that stem the ensuing year in the majority of cases. It is important that these buds make an early start to be able to complete their growth and set a flower bud for the next spring. As soon as the spent

*Very old Pink Pearl being renewed by heavy pruning.
Note fresh new growth from old wood. One more hard
pruning will bring huge trusses and restore balance*

*Effect of removing spent flower trusses: branch from
which spent flowers were removed has three flower buds;
but the branch which was allowed to set seed has none*

flower is removed the buds start to grow, in some cases
as much as three weeks earlier than in an unpinched
plant.

If you wish to convince yourself that the foregoing is
true, try a little experiment:

Remove the spent flowers from half of a plant and
leave them in place on the other half. Observe from time
to time the comparative growth of the new buds. You will
be amazed at the retarding influence the spent flower
spurs will have upon these buds, especially if seed pods
are being formed. The following year the results will be
even more in evidence. Nearly every terminal bud on the
pruned side will be a large, strong flower bud. Many, and
sometimes all, of the buds on the unpruned side will be
leaf buds only, resulting in a disappointing show.

Some hybrids have a tendency to develop more new
shoots than the branch can support. After considerable
growth, these crowded shoots do not have sufficient room
on the stem and they break down, leaving a weakened
fork and an entrance for disease spores. Three or four
new branches from the base of the old flower are sufficient. If more buds start into growth they should be
rubbed off before they can do any harm.

Renewing Old Plants

If your garden contains rhododendrons that have never
been pruned and are now too large for their surroundings
or are ungainly and starved looking, try pruning. You will
be surprised how they will respond even to a very severe

heading back into old wood. In England, during World
War II, it was found necessary to cut down rhododendron
trees that were more than a hundred years old and had
trunks more than a foot in diameter. Most of these plants
immediately stump-sprouted, and in a very short time
were fine bushy plants again, ready for another hundred
years. This shows the remarkable vitality and longevity
of the dormant buds.

In the garden, plants that grow as a clump should have
some of the oldest stems entirely removed, at which time
they will produce a crop of sturdy young shoots that will
become the plant of the future. These must be thinned
out to two or three of the strongest; and if they show
extreme vigor they must be tip-pinched at the desired
height, otherwise they may equal the height of the old
growth and nullify your objective.

Hybrids

Most of the rhododendrons sold in this country today
are hybrids, which are propagated by grafting on *R.
ponticum* rootstock. They usually have a single main
stem which branches some distance from the ground. It
would be very unwise to cut this single trunk, which, of
course, would remove the entire plant and leave only a
stump. Some stumps would sprout, it is true, but many
would fail, resulting in the loss of the plant. Such severe
pruning is seldom necessary. The heading back of any
of the laterals will produce new shoots which will effectively renew the plant. There are dormant buds near the

terminal of each season's growth. When pruning, always cut just *above* the joint which indicates one season's growth regardless of the age of the branch. What appear to be buds on the lower half of a seasonal growth section are only leaf scars that cannot produce new shoots. The new growth will then come from the previous year's growth, and the cut section will die back to this point, as shown in the drawing. In the rhododendron family the

Cut just above joint for new growth

annual growth is clearly defined, and one or ten years' growth may be removed from any lateral branch depending on how much you wish to reduce the size of your plant. If conditions are otherwise favorable, sufficient new growth is practically assured.

Heavy pruning of grafted hybrids will generally cause the *ponticum* rootstock to put forth a crop of suckers. These suckers are quite common even without stimulation. They should always be removed immediately, for if allowed to remain they will divert all food from the hybrid and rapidly overwhelm it. All rhododendrons should be examined periodically for these sucker growths, because the *ponticum* stock never loses its ability to assert itself and to try to destroy its unwelcome guest.

Himalayan Hybrids

In areas where frost is a rare occurrence, the group of white hybrid rhododendrons headed by *R. fragrantissimum* is a treasure for the acid garden. Featured in Golden Gate Park, San Francisco, they create tremendous interest in their lily-like corollas and heavenly fragrance.

This group is extremely easy to grow under conditions that are favorable to any acid-loving plant. They naturally grow in a very open, irregular manner which must be controlled before they can become good garden members. Training should start from the very beginning, and if diligently carried out throughout the first two or three years, only tip pinching with the thumb nail will be required. As soon as the plant has developed a stocky and bushy framework, the pinching should be discontinued and the plant may be allowed to bloom. An annual light

pruning after blooming will keep the plant in shape from then on. *R. fragrantissimum* makes an excellent espalier because of the long pliant growth and the good response to pruning and training.

The Triflorums

The triflorum group of rhododendron is best known by the "blue" species *R. augustinii* and its hybrids Blue Tit and Blue Diamond. There are several other fine species in this group with creamy yellow, pink, and white flowers, some of the latter heavily dotted with maroon in the throat.

They are easily propagated from cuttings and in the near future will undoubtedly receive the attention they so richly deserve. The species are also grown from seed, so, as they are always on their own roots, all new growth from below ground can be encouraged. They naturally tend to form clumps and are far more effective when grown in this manner. The older shoots, after several years of heavy bloom, become straggly and full of thin, dry, twiggy growth. Each year some of these older branches should be removed to the ground level so that the clump is constantly being renewed by new shoots. The dormant buds break freely on a healthy plant and wood of any age may be cut with good results. They will even stand shearing into a formal, compact plant if the surroundings demand it.

Dwarf Species

Another group of species rhododendrons that are slowly becoming better known are the small-leaved and dwarf species for the rock garden. This group contains the *lapponicum* series and, for the most part, are thicket or mat forming. To keep them in scale and in good health, they should be sharply headed back immediately after blooming to prevent the formation of seed capsules. They are such prodigious bloomers that seed formation is very devitalizing in the artificial conditions under which we grow them. It is not necessary, with most of these dwarf species, to remove any of the branches back to ground level. If they become too matted and untidy, with frequent appearance of dead branches, it is best to cut the entire plant just above ground level. If the general condition of the plant is good and cultural requirements have been properly met, the response will be immediate and highly satisfactory. No thinning of the new growth is required, even though it is seemingly heavy.

Deciduous Azaleas

The deciduous azaleas are among the hardiest members of the great race of rhododendrons and are well known in northern areas where the evergreen azaleas and hybrid rhododendrons are unknown. They require very little pruning beyond the removal of dead and broken branches. The tendency of some of the American species to sprawl can be corrected by heading back. This should be done immediately after the blooming season to allow the new shoots as much growing time as possible. Not only will an occasional heading back develop a more shapely and attractive plant, but it will materially increase the quantity of flowers.

Evergreen Azaleas

Little pruning is necessary in the evergreen group of azaleas except to remove damaged or diseased branches. Some heading back may be required by some of the more vigorous types, although the free use of cut sprays will generally keep the plants within bounds. Most of the popular varieties are naturally neat and compact, and they need very little training. If young plants should show a tendency to send up one or two tall, thin stems they should be pinched back to force branching near the ground. If this is done early in the growing period only the top buds may start into growth. These, too, must be pinched back until enough new branches have started to insure a bushy plant. The more lateral branches you have the greater will be the display of flowers. Pinching and pruning should be completed by midsummer so that the branches can mature and set flower buds.

Varieties that bloom near the end of the azalea season sometimes start into growth before the flower buds open. The new shoots tend to obscure the blooms and prevent enjoyment of the mass effect for which the azaleas are famous. It is perfectly safe and highly desirable to remove these shoots as soon as they begin to rise above the flower buds. The floral show will then be unobstructed, and there will be ample dormant buds to produce new wood in time to set buds for the following season.

Revitalizing Azaleas

In some areas, azaleas tend to be short-lived and after a few years to show a gradual deterioration. When such a condition becomes evident, drastic pruning is indicated. Remove the entire mass of short twiggy growth that forms in the crown of the plant. Cut out all dead, weak, and crossing branches to allow plenty of growing room for the mass of new shoots that will break from above and below ground. As soon as this new growth is well established, the old shoots that failed to break, or died part way back, can be cut away. The effect of this treatment is a revitalized plant that has many floriferous years ahead. If performed at the close of the flowering season, there is a very good chance that a display will be produced the next year.

CHAPTER 6. The Rose Garden

All roses should be pruned regardless of type, age, or use. Rose growers agree on that point, but from then on agreement is rare indeed. Each specialist has a method that he has developed for his own area and type of culture and the varieties that he favors. This is as it should be and shows an intelligent and observant approach to the problem.

The fact that so many techniques are put forward as the "only" one really serves to show what a hardy and adaptable plant the rose is. We are not concerned in this book with the hobbyist who grows many roses, usually in areas set aside for them alone. There is a generous literature on the rose which is being constantly augmented. This present work covers the fundamentals for the average gardener who has one or a few roses in mixed plantings that receive only the general care afforded such gardens. These gardeners are the ones who find it so hard to believe that in order to have good roses they must prune severely and at the proper time. Few other shrubs should have as much wood removed every year as the familiar hybrid tea roses.

When to Prune

The time of pruning is largely determined by climate.

In mild climates along the Pacific Coast and in the southern states, where hardiness is not considered, bush roses may be pruned in one operation any time during January. The middle of the month is about the best time, as it just precedes the start of new growth. Earlier pruning in November and December produces more dieback. Varieties which show this tendency at the later pruning date should have the cuts covered with a good grafting wax or pruning compound.

In areas where roses have to be covered in the winter to protect them from the cold, it is customary to cut the bushes back a third or more in late fall to prevent storm damage. The regular pruning is then performed in late March or early April, as soon as the danger of freezing is past.

Gardeners living in borderline areas and in climatic "pockets," such as mountain valleys, will have to regulate their pruning within the period between January 1 and April 15.

Amount to Prune

The amount to prune is not so simple to determine. There are two rules that form the basis for our planning:

1. The weaker the bush the harder the pruning.
2. Prune hard for size of flower and light for quantity of flowers.

Many of the older varieties of hybrid tea roses are of weak constitution and make comparatively slender branches. These varieties must be cut back severely. Leave only three to five of the strongest and youngest

canes and cut them back to two or three dormant buds. The newer varieties are much more robust and make

sturdy canes an inch or more in diameter. It would be a mistake to cut such roses back severely. They are able to produce large-sized, long-stemmed flowers from a much larger plant. These varieties may be pruned to a height of 18 inches and in extremely vigorous cases even to a greater height.

There is no exact height that is best for all varieties, and each plant should receive individual attention. They all should, of course, be thinned out to not more than five strong canes. Some laterals may be left on these high-pruned varieties if they are strong and well placed. These laterals must be headed back to a couple of strong dormant buds. Varieties that grow stiffly upright should always be pruned to outside buds in order to spread the new growth. Pruning to inside buds will make a sprawling specimen assume a more upright framework.

In each case the strong canes that are retained are able to produce good bloom for several years, and they need not be removed until they become hard and knotty and fail to produce the length of stem desired. Each year at least one of these older canes should be removed entirely. A healthy rose bush will produce more new shoots from the base than are needed for replacement.

Base Shoots and Suckers

Often, new shoots growing from the base are mistaken for suckers and are removed as soon as observed. This is a great mistake, because they are the future bush and are vitally necessary to replace the old wood removed at pruning time. Most of these shoots are quite different in appearance from the older portions of the bush, but if they come from *above* the bud union they are valuable new wood. Any growths from *below* the bud union are suckers and should be removed immediately.

If more new shoots are produced than are needed for wood renewal, they should be rubbed off while small. The remainder should be tip-pinched very lightly when about a foot tall. Hard heading at a later date will usually result in the death of the entire shoot. This tip-pinching will cause the selected shoots to develop laterals that will harden and mature within the growing season. If not headed, the shoot will continue its soft, sappy growth up through the plant without branching and be of little use to the plant. Proper handling of these new basal growths is the secret of successful rose culture. When a rose bush that is being properly watered, fed, and sprayed fails to produce basal shoots, it should be discarded.

Cutting Blossoms

The cutting of roses is a very important part of the pruning operation, whether the flower is to be used as a cut flower or removed for the sake of tidiness when it is faded. Never leave more than two mature five-parted leaves on each stem. If spent flowers are snipped off leav-

ing a long, many-leaved stem, the result will be inferior short-stemmed blooms at a later date. The shorter cut will produce two fine roses.

If the bush is for garden ornament only and length of stem is of no importance, the bush may be lightly pruned. Thin out dead or diseased wood, crossing branches, and any weak shoots that are overcrowded. Head back lightly, removing as many as possible of the "knuckles" formed by repeated removal of spent blooms. While many more canes are left, they should be renewed occasionally as described above.

Tree Roses

Tree or standard roses are regular varieties budded at the top of a single stem or "trunk," which may vary in length in different parts of the country. They must never be neglected in the pruning program, for they require careful treatment and their margin of safety is much smaller than with other forms. The pruning should be done late in the dormant season, just before new growth

starts, to prevent die-back or the entrance of disease organisms. Two or three buds may be left on each lateral produced the preceding year. A few extremely vigorous varieties could have a bit more wood left on them.

After the first crop of bloom is over, all of the new wood should be shortened back to sound buds, including the ones that flowered. These buds will in time produce a second good crop of bloom. The same procedure should be followed when these flowers have faded. All of this short twiggy growth should be pruned away during the next dormant pruning operation.

Polyantha and Floribunda Roses

The Polyantha roses are cluster-flowering, grown for mass effect, and it is not necessary to prune them as severely as the regular large-flowering hybrids. More canes can be left and the heading can be light. Remove the spent clusters back to the first strong bud. Too-vigorous shoots may be tipped at any time.

Similar treatment is afforded the increasingly popular Floribunda roses. They vary in habit, and the rule to prune according to vigor may be followed, except that they need not be pruned so severely as the teas. Some varieties require a summer pruning of the long canes that, if allowed to remain, would spoil the mass effect desired of this type of rose.

The newer, patented miniature roses are too dwarfed to prune in the regular manner, and yet they become twiggy and short stemmed in a few months. These plants are on their own roots and may be sheared off at ground level. New shoots immediately start into growth and produce flowers in a very short time. This cutting back can be repeated time after time, as soon as a heavy blooming period is past. They will then produce a good crop of charming baby roses. This method will make many friends for these little gems that might otherwise fail to impress with their elfin beauty.

Shrub Roses

The shrub roses, hybrids of *Rosa rugosa,* are lightly pruned. Simply remove the old flowering canes and head back the plant lightly. Four feet is not too high for this group, which makes them valuable as hedge plants.

Climbing Roses

There are two main groups of climbing roses. Some bloom throughout the season as do the bush varieties from which they are derived. Others bloom only once a year in the spring.

Spring Flowering. The spring-flowering varieties must not be pruned until after the blooming period is over. Then all canes that flowered must be removed, because they will not bloom again. New canes that are pushing up should be retained and trained for next season. An

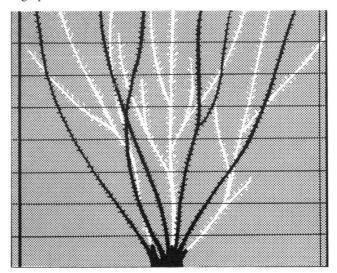

easier method is to cut off the entire plant at ground level and then thin and train the new growth that will soon follow. This cutting should be done as soon after flowering as possible, to enable the new wood to make sufficient growth before cold weather.

Everblooming. The so-called everblooming climbers are lightly pruned late in the dormant season. The main canes are lightly headed, if necessary, but all laterals should be cut back to two or three buds. Older canes that have produced for some years should be removed one or two at a time and be replaced with vigorous new canes. Remove all surplus new shoots before they can rob the plant of needed food.

Belle of Portugal seems to be in a class by itself and is so extremely vigorous that a second summer pruning must be resorted to in some cases.

Mermaid can be the exception to the rule that all roses should be pruned annually. It is a rampant trailing variety that is unsurpassed for covering slopes and banks in difficult locations. It may be left entirely to its own devices, and need not be pruned except where some control is necessary. Dead branches are rare, but should be removed if they appear.

CHAPTER 7. Ornamental Trees

Trees planted to shade a patio, screen out sun or wind, or to add color to the garden require pruning at various stages of their lives. Some need it only during their training years, some require it to keep from towering above the garden or blotting it out in shade, all need some for their own good health.

Broadleaved Evergreens

Here again we restrict ourselves to the broadleaved evergreens. The pruning of such trees used as street trees is covered in a later chapter. Our present concern is their use in the garden and as windbreaks or shade trees. As with the broadleaved evergreen shrubs, we find their greatest popularity in the far West and the southern section of the country. Not many of them are hardy to more than a few degrees of frost; consequently, they are little known in the greater portion of the United States.

How Much Pruning Needed? Most of the broadleaved evergreen species require light pruning, after the early training has produced a good, well-branched head.

As with all plants, large or small, the dead, broken, and diseased branches should be removed as soon as observed. Low branches that interfere with passage beneath them or inhibit the growth of surrounding plants should be removed. Such limbs usually sag lower and lower as they increase in length, and wiring or bracing are ugly expedients that are rarely satisfactory. Cut them off at the trunk. If cut properly, and protected with tree-wound seal, the cuts will heal very quickly and will not be objectionable.

If a low branch is badly needed and its removal would leave a gaping hole in the framework of the tree, try heading back to a good upper lateral branch or a strong bud, and train this new growth. The removal of two-thirds of the weight by thinning the laterals will sometimes permit a limb to spring back up out of the way and at the same time hasten the development of a strong lateral that will become the dominant branch when the old limb is headed back to it at a later date.

Troublemaker: Eucalyptus

In California, hundreds of thousands of eucalyptus have been planted and they have seeded themselves and become so thoroughly at home that it is hard to realize that they all came from far-off Australia. The common blue gum, *Eucalyptus globulus,* is one of the fastest growing of all trees and has been widely used as a windbreak, for erosion control and watersheds, and in the wood lot.

When in thick stands, they grow tall and straight, with comparatively small side branches. This species, as well as the other widely used varieties, such as *E. viminalis,* tends to branch out when grown separately, especially under the conditions prevailing in the fog belt along the coast.

These trees have a peculiarity which makes them very dangerous to use in play or picnic areas, unless constantly watched and heavily pruned when necessary. They grow long, spreading branches that carry an enormous weight of leaves and seed pods. In moist or rainy weather, these branches can pass through terrific wind storms without injury. Then, on a warm, sunny day, without a breeze stirring, a large branch may sometimes suddenly drop clear of the tree without warning. The branches rarely bend down gradually and hit tip first, but come down horizontally. Since the single branches may weigh several hundred pounds, they can cause serious injury to people or damage to property.

As a precautionary measure, it is sometimes advisable to stub back older trees. Fortunately, the eucalyptus has unlimited ability to initiate new growth, and it is common practice to saw off the entire head, leaving a bare trunk resembling nothing so much as a telephone pole. Within a few weeks, hundreds of new shoots break out around the top of the trunk. Gradually a few of the stronger shoots will outgrow the rest and become the main limbs of the new head. Pruning out surplus shoots will aid this process and prevent the tree from looking like a ball of green on a pole. This severe treatment rarely results in the loss of a tree; indeed, trees up to 3 feet in diameter, when cut flush with the ground, generally stump-sprout immediately and freely. The time of the year seems to make little difference to them, although late spring is recommended where borderline hardy. Of course, trained men with heavy equipment are required for this work, but it is well to know that any amount of thinning or heading is possible with the eucalyptus.

Troublemakers: Suckering Trees

There is another small group of trees with which we frequently need to take rather heroic measures. Some species of deciduous magnolias are good examples. The wood in the main trunk seems to harden prematurely, which restricts the passage of water and nutrients. The annual growth becomes short and stubby and the foliage and flowers are sparse and dwarfed. Instead of a shapely tree, it becomes a straggly bush.

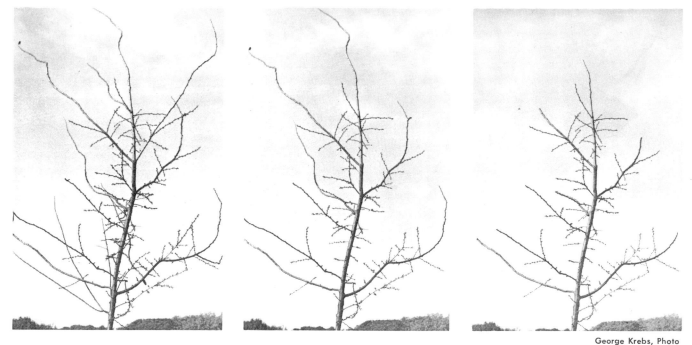

Deciduous branch before pruning   *Same branch* thinned *but not headed*   *Same branch* headed *after thinning*

Some species try to overcome this by sending out strong sucker growths from the base which will outgrow the original trunk and eventually supplant it. In gardens, all too frequently, these fine new growths are cut away on the theory that they are robbing the tree and preventing its growth. If the tree is a grafted specimen and the new growths come from *below* the graft, of course they should be removed as soon as discovered. If a strong, straight and healthy shoot should originate *above* the graft, and the main trunk is hard and stunted, save this shoot, by all means. Stake it and train it and you will soon have a far better tree than the one you started with. The old portion may be removed immediately or left until the next blooming season, when it may be cut for indoor decorations.

When these shoots do not start spontaneously, they may be forced out by cutting back the trunk a few inches above the graft. Usually, several shoots will start both above and below the graft union. All of those below the graft should be removed immediately, and those above the graft should be thinned down to two or three. As soon as development is well started and danger to the delicate young growth is past, the strongest shoot is retained and the rest removed.

Coniferous Evergreens

There are several reasons why conifers are generally overlooked in the pruning program.

The main reason, probably, is the fact that most coni-fers reach the home gardener after several years of shaping and training in a nursery. They are well-balanced and symmetrical and follow an outline that is typical of the variety. There is little the gardener needs to do for them, for it generally takes several seasons before the effect of this early training is outgrown, because of the more restrained growth of most of the cone-bearers.

After some years, the gardener often discovers that his cherished juniper or yew has overgrown its allotted space and that something must be done about it. Hardly a day goes by without someone calling a park department to offer a beautiful specimen conifer, for the digging. The desperate gardener has found that it is too costly to have the tree moved and he dislikes having to destroy it. Heavy pruning at this late date is seldom satisfactory.

Most conifers do not carry dormant buds below the foliage area; and when headed hard enough to remove this foliage, the branch will die without making any new laterals. Once the lower branches die from overcrowding, or are removed for any reason, they are gone forever. Very few conifers, with the possible exception of the yews and some of the junipers, will fill in at the bottom. The tree that has been neglected, and has grown out of shape or too large, should be removed and replaced with a well-trained young tree of a type that will not outgrow the available space.

How Much to Prune? Another reason why conifers are not pruned is the fear that the tree will bleed to death or be damaged by cutting. Much misinformation of this type is passed over back fences and many gardeners are guilty of spreading unfounded superstitions. No fears need be entertained on this account, *if the work is properly done.* Conifers can be safely pruned much harder than they ever *need* to be. Even the time of year is not quite so important as it is for many other types of plants.

When to Prune. The time of year does, however, influence the *response* to pruning. Pruning in spring before the flush of new growth starts has the least effect on the size of the plant. Early winter would have but little more effect. In the discussion below, we will give as the *best* time the period resulting in the greatest amount of dwarfing, as size control is the principal reason for trimming conifers.

Only the pines should be pruned at a definite stage of development. This stage is reached when the extended buds or "candles" are showing the tips of the new needles. These may be pinched back to any length, depending upon the amount of new growth we wish to have develop. The plant can be moulded into a desired shape by removing most of the candle in one place and little or none in another. If all of the candle is removed, no new growth will occur until the following year.

1. Fine-Foliaged Conifers. We may roughly divide the conifers into two groups, those with fine or scale-type foliage and those with coarse and long-needled foliage.

The first group contains most of the dwarf or slow growing species and varieties that are largely used as foundation plantings and near dwellings. These include the chamaecyparis and thuja as well as the hemlocks, true cypress and the junipers. The natural habit of growth is dense and compact with a multitude of small shoots making up the tips of the branches. It would be a tedious task to prune each tip individually, so it is common practice to shear them. In strictly formal areas this is a satisfactory method, and regular shearings will maintain the tailored look and keep the plant confined to a suitable size.

In the typically informal garden of today, size and compactness of conifers can be more pleasingly maintained by pinching. This may be done with the thumbnail, sharp pruning knife, or a light pair of hand-pruning

shears. Only those tips that grow out beyond the outline of the plant should be removed. Substantially the same amount of new growth is removed as in shearing, but the plant has a softer and more natural look. In both cases, the amount removed should not exceed the annual growth. It is possible to cut very close to the previous year's growth without damage, but at least a small portion of the current wood should be left.

This shearing or pinching can be done at any time during the year, when the need arises and the time is available. The *best* time is undoubtedly just as the new growth is completed in late spring or early summer. The wood is soft and cuts easily and the fresh color indicates the extent of the new growth. It is too late for the plant to put out an appreciable amount of new growth, and the buds will have time to set for growth the following year.

2. Long-Needled Conifers. The second group, composed of the pines, cedars, spruces and firs, has a definite branch pattern and fewer side branches. The buds are easily visible, but are far less numerous than in the first group. Hand shears are required and the cuts should be made just above a bud or at a crotch, as shown in the drawing.

Varieties like the true cedars build up tiers of branches that gradually force the older part of the branch down. When these branches become shaded and starved by the more vigorous top growth, they become shabby and sometimes die outright. They should be removed back to the point from which the new shoot arises.

Pruning of this group of conifers may be done at the same time as the others, when the new growth is completed. It may also be done in the winter before the buds begin to grow. The buds are easily seen at this time, so that the pruning can be used to control the new growth.

Here, more than in any other branch of pruning, should the inherent shape of the variety be followed. Train and restrain, but do not attempt to change the habit of a conifer.

Training the Young Tree

Perhaps no phase of pruning is more important, has more lasting value to the garden, and yet is more generally misunderstood and so rarely practiced, than the early training of evergreen or deciduous ornamental trees.

The old taboos against pruning, and an abiding faith in "Nature's" ability to produce perfect specimens unaided, have led many gardeners to neglect early training. In later years, the effect of this early neglect is usually a badly shaped tree that requires costly pruning and surgery or, possibly, entire removal. In addition, an improperly trained tree is vulnerable to storm damage. A tree properly trained in its early stages is far better able to withstand strong winds.

The earlier the training is started, the easier it will be, and the less pruning will be necessary through later years.

The ideal ornamental tree is one with a single, strong, straight trunk and a well-formed head. The exception to this is the tree grown solely for shade, where spread and not height is the goal. The modified-leader system of training, as used for *fruit* trees, is sometimes more suitable and is described in Chapter Eight.

A tree with a single bole, firmly rooted in a good soil, is well adapted to withstand wind and storm. The most vulnerable tree is the one with two or more main trunks. Winds whip the trunks at different angles and with varying intensities, and this stress almost inevitably causes a split at the crotch. The more exposed portion of the injured tree is usually blown down; but even if the tree remains standing, the split admits moisture, disease, and insects to the heartwood, and in a very short time causes severe trouble. Heavy bolting must be resorted to, but this is always unsightly and it only postpones the inevitable removal of the tree.

Deciduous trees and shrubs are usually sold with bare roots (no soil attached) during winter, although they may be purchased in containers at other seasons. Some deciduous plants that are known to be difficult to transplant, such as the magnolias, are balled and burlapped even for winter planting. Small conifers and practically all broadleaved evergreens are sold in containers or with an earth ball firmly burlapped and securely tied.

Pruning at Planting Time. As most of us start with trees in the smaller sizes, let us begin our training program the minute our tree is received from the nursery. Usually, nursery stock has been guided and trained to some extent before you receive it. Many nurseries sell top quality trees that require no further pruning whatever the first season.

The principle that guides the pruning of newly obtained material is the balancing of root and top systems until the tree has become established. All newly dug plants, whether they are deciduous or evergreen, have lost a good percentage of their feeder root system in the digging process. Nurserymen usually do not remove the top to make up for this loss, unless they are asked to do so. They have learned from experience that customers will hesitate to buy the cut-back plants. This, in itself, proves that a better understanding of pruning objectives is highly desirable. The removal of top wood at the time of planting is not a loss. On the contrary, it prevents die-back that could well destroy more wood and a greater number of important branches than proper pruning would remove. It also permits the early development of healthy, vigorous young shoots where they are wanted. Trees that might be injured or made unsightly by cutting back are not sold bare root by reputable nurseries.

Evergreen trees purchased from nurseries or city sales yards have usually been dug for some time and have been

R. L. Hudson, Photo

Laterals on young crab-apple tree headed to restrain growth, force formation of scaffold. Leader not headed.

Results of pruning. Note the well-placed framework branches. Cutting to outside buds spreads tree outward

CENTRAL-LEADER SYSTEM. First Pruning. *Select leader and two primary scaffolds. Head primaries below leader. If fruit tree, it would have been headed at planting*

Second Pruning. *If scaffolds not developed at right height at first pruning, select now. Head back over-developed primaries, keep leader dominant. Thin branches*

Third Pruning. *Extend framework by encouraging laterals and secondary scaffolds. Select laterals near tips of branches, a few strong ones along stem. Remove others*

Fourth Pruning. *From now on, thinning is usually sufficient. Remove watersprouts, suckers, dead wood, criss-crossing branches. Keep central leader dominant*

balled and burlapped. Or they may be growing in large tin cans or in wooden boxes. They have already re-established a balance between the roots and top, so need not be pruned back *if* the ball of earth was not broken during transportation and planting.

The plant balled to order for immediate delivery *must* be cut back. The amount to cut will vary with the size of the ball in relation to the size of the plant, the habit of the species, the season, the weather, and the stage of new growth in the individual plant. With so many factors involved, the beginner is apt to throw up his hands in utter confusion or trust to the advice of someone who frequently is as ignorant of the principles involved as he is. The lessons learned in Chapter Two combined with careful observation and a goodly portion of common sense will enable anyone to proceed without misgiving.

If the young tree is of a rapid-growing type and has many branches and a lot of soft new growth, it will need to be cut back about two-thirds. This can be accomplished by shortening in all of the branches equally and waiting until the next pruning to select the branches that will form the framework of the tree. A better way is to select the three or four main branches now and only remove their soft tips to prevent wilting. The rest of the branches may then be removed entirely or severely cut back. It has become the practice to leave a few leaves or surplus branches on the tree until the following year. They shade the tender trunk and produce food materials without competing with the selected branches.

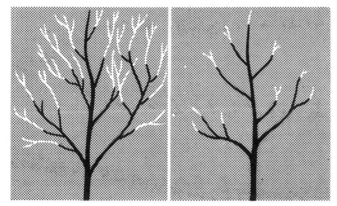

Headed two-thirds   Headed one-third

In the case of a sparsely branched tree with firm foliage, only a third or less of the top may need to be removed.

In either case, after-care is important. Shade the tree for a few days and spray with a mist spray several times a day. Watch for a severe wilt; and if the leaves do not freshen during the night, remove more wood. Two weeks of this care is usually sufficient.

Second Pruning. The second pruning is the most

important of all. The entire life of the tree is influenced by the treatment that it receives throughout its second year in the garden. Though the amount of wood removed may be very small, the effects of pruning show quickly.

A vigorous and healthy young tree planted in rich, well-prepared soil and carefully watered and maintained, will generally respond to pruning with a luxuriant mass of new shoots and foliage. If we selected our framework branches at planting time and have practiced tip-pinching or tip-pruning throughout the summer, there will be little to do at the end of the first year. That little is very important and it should not be neglected just because our young tree looks so healthy.

Frame branches selected the first year usually make more growth than their slender limbs can support. These must be lightened, or the entire branch will either break off or droop. If a wide and open type of tree is desired, leave the terminal shoot on these secondary branches and remove most of the stronger lateral shoots. If a strong, compact tree is the goal, remove the terminal back to well-placed tertiary laterals which will then become the framework branches.

A tree having long, soft, willowy branches and a weak trunk should be treated differently. In addition to the firm staking necessary to train this type of tree, the framework branches should, in most cases, be delayed until the trunk has a chance to develop sufficient strength to support them. Keep heading back all of the side branches, but leave as much foliage as possible to keep the root system vigorous and to provide food to build up the weak trunk. Then, in the second summer pruning or the third winter pruning, select the permanent framework to be allowed to develop.

Regardless of the type of tree or the time of pruning, *never* allow more than one main leader to form. Even when trained by the modified-leader system, the tree will look more natural and have a stronger framework if the modified leader remains dominant at all times. Generally, several of the upper branches of a rapidly growing young tree will strive for dominance. Because of ample food and water and plenty of light, these branches are able to grow equally and evenly. We must control this by selecting the straightest and best-placed of these for the main trunk, and by heading back all of the others repeatedly until the selected branch has undisputed dominance. If any of the others grow close to the selected leader and form a tight angle with it, they must be removed entirely. Once the leader is established, it rarely requires later assistance. Unless damaged, it will stay out in front of all rivals.

Third and Fourth Prunings. In the third and fourth years, with the leader well established, the training of the side branches takes priority.

If we wish rapid upward growth to provide high shade for rhododendrons, fuchsias, et cetera, we must remove the lower limbs and thin out the upper ones to throw all the strength of the tree into the main framework branches. This will occur naturally if we fail to do so, but it takes many years and a great deal more work later on in removing the accumulated dead branches. Also, this wastes a large amount of plant food that might have gone into developing the upper part of the tree.

In Chapter Two we learned that a tree may grow longitudinally only in the bud area. A branch leaving the trunk at 4 feet from the ground will always be exactly that same distance from the ground. Obviously, if you want a tree ultimately to shade a patio, with the lowest limb 6 feet from the ground, and the tree from the nursery was only 5 feet overall when you planted it, you must pinch and train to reach your goal. No side limb may be permitted to remain until the tree has made a growth permitting branches to form at the 6-foot level. We repeat, however, that the quickest and best method is to pinch back the tips of all unwanted side shoots for the first few years, rather than to remove them entirely. Later on the shade of the crown will eliminate them.

Continue the training of the main scaffold branches as long as they can be reached conveniently. Develop well-placed secondary branches and tip back those that are too rank or poorly placed.

This may sound like a lot of work, but the work actually required to train an individual tree in this manner amounts to no more than a couple of hours per year. A stout thumbnail, sharp knife, or a light pair of shears, used throughout the entire season, makes this training a pleasant garden activity instead of a chore. It allows the plant to make maximum use of food materials, and it eliminates the bobbed or pruned look objected to by so many gardeners. A "little and often" is far better than a "lot but seldom."

Training for Low-Headed Form. The above training is suggested for trees that are to be headed high so that the lowest branches will clear anyone or anything that might pass beneath them. Many trees are planted for screens or windbreaks, and for such use would be headed very low. Heading the newly planted tree back to 12 or 18 inches would insure a good supply of laterals from which to choose the framework. The top branch would become the new leader and pinching and pruning could then proceed as for the standard tree.

Training Subtropicals

We referred, some time back, to the dumpy and shrub-like appearance of trees from warmer and wetter sections of the globe. The above described training may have to be carried on for several more years before such a plant may be left to its own devices. The removal of lower branches, the rather heavy thinning program, the heading back of lateral branches, and the insistence on a single main trunk, all tend to force our reluctant captive "up in the world." This training, coupled with a balanced feeding program and copious watering, generally makes these species assume their normal tree-like habit.

Digest of Pruning Requirements

The following section lists alphabetically most of the trees that one may expect to find in general nurseries. As this listing is intended primarily for the amateur and the home gardener, it omits the rare and exotic. Pruning techniques for fruit trees are discussed in detail in Chapter Eight.

It is strongly advised that you study the preceding text before using the abbreviated information that follows. Once basic knowledge is acquired, a quick reference to the notes that follow should supply all the clues needed for pruning an unfamiliar tree.

May we emphasize that the following instructions indicate what *may* be done, not necessarily what *must* be done. You are the only judge of that. It is true that all ornamental trees require careful training in their first few years in the garden, but after the fourth year, most of them require little further care, except to control size and shape.

A few trees require pruning as a condition for good bloom or generous foliage; some require severe pruning for restraint. These conditions are noted in the listing.

The best time for pruning is indicated under "Mild" for areas that have little or no frost, under "Cold" for localities where freezing is the rule. The fine points of timing must be determined by experience in your own locality.

It should be understood that a tree described as "requiring no pruning" must have dead, diseased, broken, or criss-crossing branches removed as soon as they are discovered.

The term "training only" applies to those trees that require a helping hand only through their first critical years in the garden. Once the framework is established, pruning of these trees can usually be discontinued except to control size and shape.

The term "cutting to spurs" means the heading back of a lateral that is young, strong, and well-placed, to a good bud near the parent branch. It is used for wood renewal.

Acacia (tree types)

Habit: Spreading, rapid. *Train:* Specimen, street tree. Needs heavy staking and careful training while small.

Will produce more foliage than trunk can support. *Prune:* Thin heavily and tip lightly until head is formed. Will stand very heavy pruning where necessary. Mild: Fall for foliage types, after flowering for flowering types.

Acer   *Maple*

Habit: Spreading, open. *Train:* Specimen, street tree. *Prune:* Well-mannered trees that require little pruning after the training years. Do not prune in spring because of a tendency to bleed profusely. Mild: Fall. Cold: Fall or early summer.

Alnus   *Alder*

Habit: Compact. *Train:* Specimen. Train while young to single trunk. *Prune:* Remove suckers. Thin weak branches until strong framework is formed. Use cones and catkins for indoor decoration. Mild or cold: While dormant.

Arbutus Menziesii   *Madrone*

Habit: Compact, round-headed. *Train:* Specimen. *Prune:* Little pruning required, but may be headed if necessary. Avoid cutting back, which gives a clumsy, stubby effect. Mild: When growth starts in spring.

Betula   *Birch*

Habit: Open, arching. *Train:* Specimen, woodland. *Prune:* Training only. Prevent branches of equal size from forming narrow crotches. Do not prune in spring because of a tendency to bleed. Mild or cold: Fall or early summer.

Cercidiphyllum

Habit: Neat, upright. *Train:* Specimen. *Prune:* Training only.

Conifers   *Cone-bearing evergreens*

See page 45.

Cornus (tree forms)   *Dogwood*

Habit: Open. *Train:* Specimen, natural. *Prune:* Early shaping and training. Keep heading to a minimum.

Cotinus   *Smoke-tree*

Habit: Compact large shrub or small tree. *Train:* Specimen, natural. *Prune:* Training only. Spent flower heads may be removed if desired.

Crataegus   *Hawthorn*

Habit: Small compact trees. *Train:* Specimen, street tree, large hedge. *Prune:* Train to single leader. Thin out head. Use flowers and/or fruit for decoration. Remove all suckers. Will stand severe heading and pruning where necessary. Mild or cold: After flowering for double flowering varieties. While dormant for fruiting varieties.

Eriobotrya   *Loquat*

Habit: Neat, compact, round-headed. *Train:* Specimen. *Prune:* Thin the branches if the growth is too dense to permit light to reach center of tree. If grown for fruit, prune out one-half of each flower cluster. This results in a marked improvement in the fruit. Mild: Thinning should be done in the fall.

Eucalyptus   *Gum*

Habit: Rapid, weak, spreading. *Train:* Specimen, street tree, tall windbreak. *Prune:* Needs pruning, training and staking in young stages to become tree. May be pruned as hard as desired. Will generally stump-sprout even if killed or cut off at ground level. Mild: After flowering or spring.

Fagus   *Beech*

Habit: Open-headed tree. *Train:* Specimen, large hedge. *Prune:* Training during formative years only.

Fraxinus   *Ash*

Habit: Symmetrical. *Train:* Specimen, street tree. *Prune:* Early training only. Mild or cold: Fall.

Fraxinus uhdei   *Evergreen or shamel ash*

Habit: Tall, slender. *Train:* Specimen, street tree. *Prune:* Shaping and training only. Fall or spring.

Ginkgo biloba   *Maidenhair-tree*

Habit: Neat, upright. *Train:* Specimen, street tree. *Prune:* Early training only.

Gleditsia   *Honey locust*

Habit: Loose, graceful head. *Train:* Specimen, large barrier hedge. *Prune:* Prune and thin heavily to prevent breakage. Mild or cold: Fall.

Grevillea robusta   *Silk-oak*

Habit: Slender, graceful, feathery. *Train:* Specimen, street tree. *Prune:* Early training in late spring.

Halesia   *Great silver-bell*

Habit: Compact. *Train:* Specimen. *Prune:* Training only.

Harpullia

Habit: Dense, round-headed. *Train:* Specimen. *Prune:* Light thinning and clean-up in spring.

Hoheria

Habit: Upright with pendulous branches. *Train:* Specimen, copse. May be trained as a many-stemmed clump. Best when trained to a single leader or trunk. Side branches must be headed if an upright framework is desired. *Prune:* Once established, pruning may be discontinued. Mild: After flowering.

Hymenosporum flavum   *Sweet-shade*

Habit: Open, slender. *Train:* Specimen. *Prune:* Training only.

Jacaranda

Habit: Round headed. *Train:* Specimen. *Prune:* Small inner branches die back and should be removed.

Koelreuteria   *Goldenrain-tree*

Habit: Open, spreading. *Train:* Specimen. *Prune:* Little pruning after early training. Removal of spent flowers prevents the formation of unsightly pods. After flowering.

Laburnum   *Golden-chain*

Habit: Erect trunk, willowy branches. *Train:* Specimen, wall shrub. *Prune:* Light shaping. Mild or cold: After flowering.

Lagerstroemia   *Crape-myrtle*

Habit: Round-headed. *Train:* Specimen. May be trained as a large shrub or as a standard tree. *Prune:* Prune heavily to develop new wood.

Liquidambar   *Sweet gum*

Habit: Thick, pyramidal. *Train:* Specimen, street tree. Keep central leader dominant. *Prune:* For the first two or three years, thin to well-placed branches to develop a strong crown.

Liriodendron tulipifera   *Tulip-tree*

Habit: Neat, compact. *Train:* Specimen, street tree. *Prune:* Training only.

Lyonothamnus   *Catalina ironwood*

Habit: Neat, compact, pyramidal. *Train:* Specimen. *Prune:* Prune for shape only. May be trained as a tree or many-stemmed shrub. Will stand severe pruning and will stump-sprout. Mild: Spring and summer.

Magnolia

Habit: Sprawling, irregular. *Train:* Specimen, wall or espalier. *Prune:* Cut as little as possible, but some control is necessary. Remove all suckers if top is satisfactory. If growth is hard and stunted, train the strongest sucker from *above the graft* and later remove the old portion of the plant. Do this only while plant is young. Mild or cold: After flowering.

Magnolia   *Evergreen types*

Habit: Compact, round-headed. *Train:* Specimen. *Prune:* Thin out while young to reduce weight and prevent storm damage. Establish good framework and lighten branches so they will not droop. Breaks well from old wood. Large branches may be removed for decoration any time of the year without damage.

Malus (various species and hybrids)   *Flowering crab-apple*

Training and control only. Use of flowers will thin sufficiently.

Maytenus

Habit: Upright with arching branches. *Train:* Specimen, copse. *Prune:* Will stand any amount of pruning and shaping. Suckers heavily. These should be removed or thinned if thick clump is desired. Mild: Fall or spring.

Melia   *Umbrella-tree*

Habit: Compact, round-headed. *Train:* Specimen, street tree. *Prune:* Needs little pruning.

Morus   *Mulberry*

Habit: Round-headed. *Train:* Specimen. *Prune:* Training only.

Myoporum

Habit: Dome-shaped. *Train:* Specimen, mass, windbreak. *Prune:* Remove frosted tips when they occur and keep center free of dead wood and weak branches. Will stand any degree of pruning and will produce shoots on wood of any age. Plants up to 6-foot height can easily be moved, if all the leaves and year-old wood are cut away. This type of pruning produces a beautiful, sturdy, compact plant which otherwise is inclined to be somewhat straggly. As the wood is soft and brittle, at least one such severe pruning is highly recommended.

Olea   *Olive*

Habit: Compact, twiggy. *Train:* As tree or shrub, hedge. *Prune:* Will stand heavy pruning and shaping. Mild: Fall or spring.

Oxydendrum   *Sour-wood*

Habit: Compact, slow. *Train:* Specimen. *Prune:* Clean up while dormant. No pruning required.

Two-year-old tree ready for second pruning. Upright habit of tree suggests training it in open-center form

As pruned, tree will develop laterals for framework, more pleasing shape. In-growing branches will be cut

Pistacia   *Pistache*

Habit: Open-headed. *Train:* Specimen. *Prune:* Training only.

Platanus   *Plane-tree*

Habit: Round-headed. *Train:* Specimen, street tree. *Prune:* Stands the heaviest pruning of any large deciduous tree. May be headed annually to one bud of the new growth. A handsome tree when properly trained and pruned thereafter. Mild or cold: Fall.

Populus   *Poplar, cottonwood, aspen*

Habit: Most cultivated varieties spire-like. *Train:* Specimen, tall screen. *Prune:* Wood is soft and liable to breakage. Should be topped out before too old. Need annual root pruning if near drains or choice garden areas. Will stand heavy pruning and heading. Mild or cold: Fall.

Prunus Amygdalus   *Flowering almond*

Use flowers freely. Remove all flowering wood back to short spurs. Cut out a few of the oldest "knuckles" each year. Mild or cold: After flowering.

Prunus Mume   *Flowering Apricot*

Restrained growth makes pruning unnecessary. Leave all current growth possible. Cut flowers from two-year-old wood leaving laterals intact. Mild or cold: After flowering.

Prunus (several species and hybrids)   *Flowering cherry*

Do not prune unless absolutely necessary. Always cut to laterals, as stubs break poorly. An opening made in the framework may never fill in. Flowers may be cut judiciously, but always to a lateral. In moist areas of summer fog, it is sometimes necessary to slash the bark to help prevent sour sap. Corrective pruning should be done in *midsummer* after new growth has slowed down.

Prunus Persica   *Flowering peach*

Cut all year-old wood back to 4-inch spurs to help prevent curly-leaf. The peach responds well to this treatment with ample quantities of fine new flowering wood. Dwarf and weeping types should not be pruned so severely. Mild or cold: During and immediately after flowering.

Prunus cerasifera   *Flowering plum*

Train to develop good framework. Prevent double leaders and congested branching. Summer tipping and pruning strongly advised to prevent watersprouts and weak growth. Mild or cold: Main pruning after flowering.

Quercus   *Oak*

Habit: Upright, spreading. *Train:* Specimen. *Prune:* The deciduous species resent pruning and should only be trained. The evergreen species will stand fairly heavy pruning where necessary. Scrubby inner branches and sucker growths should be removed. Mild or cold: Fall.

Robinia   *Black locust, False acacia*

Habit: Plume-like crown. *Train:* Specimen, large barrier hedge, street tree. *Prune:* Training only, but will stand heavy pruning. Remove suckers, which are freely borne, unless plant used as a hedge. Mild or cold: Fall.

Salix   *Pussy willow, Weeping willow*

Habit: Upright. *Train:* Specimen. *Prune:* Remove as many of the flowering shoots as desired. As soon as bloom is past, cut back all flowering shoots to short spurs. This produces vigorous new shoots for the following spring.

Twig species are clump-forming and are grown as a copse. In spring, all growth is cut back to short spurs to produce as many young highly colored shoots as possible.

The weeping willow has very soft wood, but early pruning should develop a strong framework. A few or all of the whip-like branches may be removed to encourage fresh new growth, if desired.

Schinus   *Pepper-tree*

Habit: Round-headed, drooping branches. *Train:* Specimen, street tree. *Prune:* Training only.

Sophora   *Pagoda-tree*

Habit: Round-headed, spreading. *Train:* Specimen. Train while young to establish a good framework. *Prune:* Light clean-up after flowering. Pods may be removed, but not essential.

Sorbus   *Dogberry, Rowan-tree, Mountain-ash*

Habit: Erect with drooping branches. *Train:* Specimen. *Prune:* Training only.

Sparmannia africana

Habit: Lush, soft, clump-forming. *Train:* Specimen. tub plant. *Prune:* May be left unpruned or can be headed to any desired height. Will stump-sprout if frozen or cut to the ground. Mild: Late spring.

Ulmus   *Elm*

Habit: Graceful, open. *Train:* Specimen, street tree. *Prune:* A beautiful tree if trained while young and then allowed to develop naturally, without pruning. However, it will stand any amount of pruning—a useful trait where size must be radically curtailed. Mild or cold: Fall.

Umbellularia   *California-bay, California-laurel, Pepperwood, Spice-tree, Oregon-myrtle*

Habit: Compact, round-topped. *Train:* Specimen, tub plant, hedge. *Prune:* Prune for shape. Can stand any amount of pruning or shearing. Will stump-sprout. Mild: Spring and summer.

Vitex Agnus-castus   *Hemp-tree, Chaste-tree*

Habit: Open. *Train:* Specimen. *Prune:* Prune back hard to encourage new wood. If bloom spikes are removed, a second crop will be produced in the fall. In cold areas, the entire top will freeze but will rapidly regrow from roots. Mild or cold: While dormant.

Vitex lucens   *New Zealand chaste-tree*

Habit: Bushy. *Train:* Specimen. *Prune:* Clean-up only.

CHAPTER 8. Fruit Trees

Pruning is an essential practice wherever good fruit is grown, and it requires not only a thorough understanding of the fundamentals discussed in Chapter Two, but also a specific knowledge of the species or variety at hand. The well-known orchard trees vary to a marked degree in their fruiting habits and they thus require individual treatment.

During the training period, most species receive similar handling. The little trees are encouraged to form sturdy trunks, and their laterals are usually trained by the modified-leader system to develop a well-formed head.

Once the trees reach bearing age, however, similarities in handling vanish. In order to produce large, well-formed, highly colored fruit, free of bug or blemish, the average fruit tree must be pruned each year of its bearing life. Nut trees—almond, walnut, and pecan—do not always require this annual pruning; commercial growers sometimes prune them every other year.

We can learn a great deal about the pruning of fruit trees from the orchardists who depend for their livelihood on the production of their trees. However, many of their practices are aimed at the encouragement of maximum fruit production without regard for some of the characteristics that appeal to the home gardener. Many orchard trees, for example, are trained so that their lower branches are relatively close to the ground to facilitate fruit harvesting, but the gardener usually has too little free space in his garden to give to a tree that he cannot walk under. Furthermore, some forms of commercial pruning give the tree an awkward form that would not look appropriate in a garden where it must double as an ornamental specimen.

The home gardener usually has to strike a compromise between having a tree that produces bountifully and one that is attractive in his garden. If he wishes to have his single apple tree serve as a shade tree in his outdoor living room, he will train it to a high head, even though picking the apples will be a difficult task. Should he also insist on an open, clean-limbed center with only a canopy of leaves, he will never *get* many apples, because he will have pruned away the fruit spurs.

Whether you have a single tree or a hundred, you must learn the fruiting habits of each variety before you can prune intelligently.

A word of warning: If your trees do not bear fruit, the difficulty may be one that cannot be corrected by pruning. Some fruits will not bear unless conditions are exactly to their liking. For instance, some will not ripen in the coastal fog belt because of the lack of continuous sunshine. Often, a tree that will prosper in one locality will barely survive in another only fifty miles away, because of differences in soil or climatic conditions.

Absence of fruit may also be caused by the need of a particular species for cross-pollination. Some fruits must be planted in pairs in order to bear.

Early Training

There are three principal methods of training young pre-bearing fruit trees: the central-leader, modified-leader, and open-center systems.

Central-Leader Training

The "central-leader" system of training fruit trees is the same as that used for ornamental trees, as described in Chapter Seven on page 47. It was at one time a fairly popular method, but it is now confined largely to walnuts, pecans, and some tropical fruits. It has gone out of favor for orchard use because the tall, pyramidal shape it produces makes it difficult for orchard crews to spray the trees or pick the fruit. It also tends to shade out the lower areas and reduce the bearing area.

In the home garden, however, this method may have some appeal to the gardener who is interested in a fruit tree for its ornamental value, who does not mind the extra clambering necessary to harvest the crop, and who does not object to the added difficulty of pruning, thinning, and spraying the tree as it grows taller. As a matter of fact, it is a valuable practice in regions with heavy snowfall, for the trees thus trained are less subject to breakage. Most fruit trees can be successfully trained in this manner, although the peach and nectarine do not look as attractive when brought up this way.

Modified-Leader Training

The "modified-leader" system of training is the one most used at the present time and has much to recommend it.

Planting Time: Most year-old trees from the nursery, with the exception of the apple and walnut, should be headed back at planting time to 24 to 30 inches from the ground, and all side branches should be removed. This will cause many of the dormant buds near the top to start into vigorous growth. All of these new shoots should be allowed to develop until the first pruning.

First Pruning: This pruning is a critical one because it determines the ultimate form of the tree. Selection of leader and scaffold branches should be made in winter or in early summer, and the balance lightly tipped back.

Choose the scaffold branches carefully. Remember that they will always be exactly the same height from the ground, and you must determine what height is the most desirable in your particular situation. Trees that grow stiffly upright, like the sweet cherry and some pears, can be headed quite low. Others, like the apple, should have their lowest limb about 3 feet from the ground, so should be headed at planting time to not less than 4 feet in height.

Second Pruning: Two primary scaffold branches, in addition to the new leader, should be selected at the second pruning if not already selected and encouraged by summer pruning. Regardless of the time of selection, the ideal primary branches should join the main trunk at a wide angle to prevent crowding. They should originate at least 6 inches apart on the trunk and should be about 120 degrees apart from each other and from the leader. From the top, the tree would resemble three evenly-placed spokes radiating from a central axle.

The leader should be headed back in proportion to the vigor of the young tree. Three feet may be left on an average tree and a bit more for a strong, straight leader that is not inclined to droop. In any case the two selected primary branches *must* be headed to a point a few inches lower than the top of the leader. This will insure dominance of the leader which must be maintained at all times. All other shoots and branches should be removed.

Should the crotches be tight and the primary branches too close together, as in sweet cherry or some varieties of pear, it would be wise to use spreaders. These are easily made from the trimmings by twisting two whips together for each spreader and using them to force each branch away from its neighbor, as shown in the drawing.

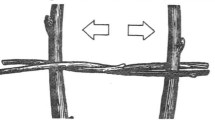

During the second year, the tree will usually put out several strong new shoots near the top of each of the headed primaries and many weaker shoots throughout their length and also on the lower trunk. This varies with the species. If desired, they may all be allowed to grow until the following fall pruning.

The better way, in the home orchard, is to start pinching the new shoots as soon as they have reached a length of 3 or 4 inches. Allow a strong tip shoot and two or three well-placed laterals to develop unchecked, and pinch back the rest. An inspection should be made in a month to see if a second pinching is necessary. The earlier this pinching is done, the less will be the dwarfing effect on the tree. By midsummer all pinching should cease, unless a definite dwarfing is desired.

Third Pruning: If the tree has not been trained by summer pinching, it will require pruning at the end of its second year in the garden. This will consist almost entirely of thinning out surplus shoots and branches.

To extend the framework, select the strongest and best-placed lateral near the tip of each primary. Select one or two well-placed secondary branches on each primary. Remove all the other strong shoots, but allow the weak ones to remain to shade the trunk and produce food. Unless they are extremely long and whip-like, the selected branches need not be headed back. Should they tend to outgrow the leader, however, they must either be headed or thinned back to a good lateral. Should the leader be unduly vigorous it may have to be checked. For instance, it is frequently necessary to head it back on the sweet cherry to force it to branch.

It may be well to emphasize how important it is to select the proper framework branches. They form the permanent structure that supports our tree throughout its entire life, and once established cannot be modified to any great degree. The natural habit of the tree and the form you wish it to take are the determining factors. Some varieties of pear should always have an outward growing lateral retained for a secondary branch because of the rigidly upright habit. Many apples have such a spreading habit that only the inward growing laterals should be selected, unless a very wide-spreading and eventually a weeping tree is the desired objective.

Thinning is all that is required from now until the tree is in full bearing. Keep the leader dominant. Keep the center of the tree open. Maintain good spacing between the branch systems so that light and air can get to them and set flowering spurs. Maintain a pleasing balance and prevent any branch from breaking the symmetry of the tree. Do not remove the small weak growths in the center and lower portions of the tree. They shade the branches, produce food, and frequently bear the best crops of fruit during the early years. Any shoots that develop too rapidly may be tip-pinched during summer, which will slow them down without robbing the tree of valuable carbohydrates.

All of the pruning mentioned above should be done as lightly as proper training will permit. Heavy pruning dwarfs the tree and delays the formation of fruit. Never remove a branch or a leaf without a well-founded reason for doing so. Each leaf is busily manufacturing food to hasten the maturity and fruitfulness of our trees.

MODIFIED-LEADER SYSTEM. First Pruning. *Select scaffold branches at proper height for particular tree; choose new leader, if developed; head scaffolds below it*

Second Pruning. *If suitable scaffolds not developed at time of first pruning, select now. Otherwise, head the primaries below leader, head leader if it is too strong*

Third Pruning. *Extend framework by encouraging laterals. Select strongest and best near top of each primary and one or two down branch. Thin other strong shoots*

Fourth Pruning. *From now on, thinning alone is usually sufficient. Remove watersprouts, suckers, dead wood, crossing branches. Keep center open, leader dominant*

Open-Center Training

At present the "open-center" method of training is used only for peach, nectarine, and almond, but most of the older orchards along the Pacific Coast are of this type.

In this type of training, the branches all originate from a small area on the main trunk which sometimes causes water pockets to form, followed by heart rot and breakdown of the weak crotches. A *delayed open-center* closely approaches the modified-leader method described above in that it takes more than one year to select the main scaffold branches. This permits better placement and the avoidance of pockets. The topmost of the three primary scaffold branches should be allowed to grow a bit higher than the other two or eventually it may be choked out. The training of the scaffolds leaves the center of the tree free of branches.

The true open-center method is one in which the main scaffold branches are selected at one time. The nursery tree is headed back at planting time to the desired height. The following winter three well-placed branches are selected, but because of the low heading desirable for peaches and the crowding of the shoots at the top of the headed trunk, these primary branches are crowded together with the undesirable results described above. Because the peach is a comparatively short-lived tree this is not too serious, but the delayed open-center system is still to be preferred. These three branches are lightly headed *evenly* so that the top one will not become dominant and all three will develop at the same rate.

In the following years, it is only necessary to keep selecting well-placed laterals and to keep the center open. The balance of the scaffolds should be kept even by heading lightly when necessary.

Almond

Most of the almond crop is borne on short spurs that have a bearing life of about five years. The annual branches also produce a few fruits. The open-center or delayed open-center system of training is a satisfactory one. Very little pruning is necessary after the framework is established in the first two or three seasons. Heading should be discontinued after the second pruning. The sparse foliage, the light weight of the crop, and the method of harvesting make it unnecessary to thin as much as for most other crops, and the tree can be allowed to reach a greater height.

The one important task, after the tree has been bearing for a few years, is to renew one-fifth of the fruit spurs annually. This is done by removing some of the smaller branches up to 1½ inches in diameter to stimulate new growth that will produce fruiting spurs. If larger branches are removed, or the heading or thinning is too severe, the almond is inclined to produce many watersprouts. These may be tipped back in early summer or removed entirely. They must not be allowed to develop, unless needed to replace a broken limb, in which case they can be trained in the same manner as the original scaffold branches.

If the growth of the young tree is excessive and flowering is delayed, do not increase the amount of pruning and heading. On the contrary, stop all pruning until the tree starts to flower. If the tree flowers but does not set fruit, pollination is at fault. All almonds must be cross-pollinated in order to bear.

Very old and tall trees that have started to go back can be renewed by drastically heading back the entire top to large sound laterals. If fertilizing and watering follow this treatment, good new growth may be expected. Check the watersprouts or thin them until just enough are left to produce a new crown.

Apple

The modified-leader type of training is the best for the apple, but the central-leader system is much used. The growth is inclined to spread the framework, hence the tree should be encouraged to grow strongly upright for the first few years. Otherwise the weight of the fruit will cause the branches to droop and become a nuisance. Always have the lowest branch at least 3 feet from the ground; and if the tree is for ornament and shade, even higher heading would be desirable.

Keep the scaffold branches as far apart on the trunk as possible. If less than 8 inches apart, they become too crowded in a few years and prevent the fruit from ripening and coloring properly. The red varieties particularly need plenty of light.

Most of the fruit is borne at the ends of short spurs that form on the branches that are two years old or more.

These spurs can produce good fruit for many years, though some varieties have a tendency to bear very lightly one season and heavily the next. Fruit growers recognize this alternate-bearing tendency, but the amateur gardener frequently cuts off these spurs, if they miss fruiting, in the mistaken belief that they have become barren. In California, the long growing season encourages the setting of new fruit buds on the bearing spur, hence many trees that would be alternate-bearing in the North and East will bear annually here.

A few varieties bear quite freely on the tips of the last year's branches and most kinds produce some fruit on year-old wood. Regardless of this, the new growth should be thinned out on bearing trees to encourage the development of new fruit spurs on the older wood and aid them to bear regularly. If this is not done, the fruit spurs will be shaded out and the crop will be borne too high in the tree.

The amount of pruning for the alternate-bearing varieties depends on the cycle of bearing. Little pruning is needed in the low-yield year beyond some thinning of the new growth. When a heavy set is expected, spurs can be pruned to prevent over-bearing and the necessity of thinning the crop. Very old spurs can be removed or cut back to the newer portions. This would also be the time to remove any branches that are drooping too low.

Most varieties of apple will produce risers (vertical shoots) along the top side of the main branches, especially after several years of heavy bearing have caused the scaffold branches to droop. Most of these should be removed as they form, except for the one that must be retained to supplant the branch after it has passed its peak of productivity. The selected shoot should be about 6 feet from the main trunk and should be trained for one to three years before the removal of the main branch becomes necessary. The selected riser should not be headed, and laterals from it should be selected with the same care as with the original limb. This renewal should be gradual and only one, or at the most two, large branches should be removed at one pruning; otherwise, suckers and watersprouts will become numerous.

Laterals should be renewed in the same manner, once they have begun to droop below the point of their origin.

It should be unnecessary, by this time, to mention that the removal of the larger limbs should be very carefully done. All cuts should be made close to the base of the new branch without leaving a stub. If the cut branch is over an inch in diameter, it should be painted with a good tree-wound seal. Leaving a stub to be removed later is of doubtful value, for if later removal is neglected, the tree is likely to suffer serious damage.

Apricot

Heavy pruning of the apricot is essential to insure regular fruit production. One-year-old shoots produce a portion of the crop, but short-lived spurs carry the major portion. As these spurs are usually good for only three years, they must constantly be renewed. The tree, in suitable areas, is a very lush grower and a heavy bearer. Unless kept in severe check, it will rapidly become too large and will bear its fruit high in the tree where it cannot be thinned or picked easily. The lower spurs will be shaded out by the lush foliage and new ones will not form. In short, you would have a fine shade tree but a very unsatisfactory fruit tree. The necessary pruning for good fruit production does not always develop a graceful garden tree.

The young tree should be trained by the modified-leader system. The selected framework branches should not be headed too severely during the training period because a wide-spreading head is desired. After the tree has reached fruiting age, it will have to be severely thinned and headed annually. No long, thin branches are left, and the pruned tree has a stubby look when properly treated. The severity of this pruning is comparative only in relation to that used for apples and pears. An earlier practice of cutting back to 4- or 6-inch stubs is rapidly being replaced by a more liberal policy of removing one-third to one-half of the new wood. This allows more room for the development of new fruiting spurs and prevents the fruit from bunching.

In the warmer inland valleys, a still longer pruning is considered best. This provides protection for the branches from a too-ardent sun and yet admits enough light to encourage the formation of new fruit spurs in the interior of the trees.

By the time the spurs are three years old, a new branch should be selected to replace the one carrying the aging spurs. The fourth season the old branch is removed entirely, and the fruit is then borne on the new branch. This process goes on constantly, from a quarter to a third of the older lateral branches being renewed each year so that the yield is not materially affected.

In the home orchard this phase need not be taken too seriously, because a tree properly trained and kept open in the center will produce enough new wood to insure a good crop for many years. As wood removal is primarily a thinning process, proper attention must be given to thinning as well as to heading.

Old trees that are not producing enough new fruiting spurs must be more drastically dealt with, although they are subject to rots and bacterial gummosis, and large cuts should be avoided if possible. If the tree has been severely pruned for years, it has been prevented from forming good laterals, so the rejuvenation process must take more than one season. Select well-situated shoots to be retained for the new branches and head back the ends of the old branches. The following year the old branch can be removed entirely, back to the base of the strong new lateral. This is similar to the renewing of fruiting wood except that it is on a larger scale, involving larger and older branches.

Avocado

The avocado has become a very important commercial crop in areas where the temperature does not drop below 26 degrees. It makes a beautiful specimen tree and is worth growing for its lush tropical appearance. The seedlings so frequently seen are usually worthless for fruit and have a rank and ungainly habit of growth. Grafted varieties are more bushy and compact and well worth the price asked for them. Varieties differ in habit. Some are spreading and others are upright. To aid in harvesting fruit and to prevent storm damage, the trees are usually headed low and then allowed to develop naturally. If upward growth is still too rapid at the expense of the laterals, further heading is required. All pruning cuts should be sealed. Trim out weak and poorly placed branches and keep the center from becoming congested. Carefully avoid leaving large openings in the canopy of leaves as the bark is thin and it sunburns easily.

Cherry

The sweet and sour cherries are usually treated separately in the literature because of their diverse cultural requirements. For our present purpose they may be considered together, because their fruiting habits are the same and, consequently, the same pruning technique is applicable to each tree.

Cherries require less wood renewal than any other fruit tree, because they bear their fruit laterally on short spurs which have a productive life of twelve years or more. Not more than 10 per cent of the bearing wood should be replaced annually. Never head back and leave a stub on large, bearing cherry trees. They do not break as freely as most trees and many dead stubs will result. Always prune to a lateral, if at all possible.

The sweet cherry grows stiffly upright and the sour cherry grows in a spreading and irregular fashion. We must bear this in mind during the training years of our young tree. The sweet cherry should have the upright shoots removed back to laterals that are growing out from the tree. This will spread the framework and allow light and air to penetrate the head of the tree. During the rapidly growing phase of the young tree, some varieties refuse to make a single lateral in the proper area for good framework, but will continue to make strong upright growth. After two or three years, these long whip-like branches will only make laterals near the tip. In such cases it becomes necessary to head back new growth to encourage branching, just above the place where the branches are desired. This is followed by a thinning out of undesirable shoots.

Summer pinching is especially valuable the first two or three years with vigorously growing trees. It encourages branching without danger of dead stubs, and if properly done will aid in training the tree to a more open head with better spread.

Reverse this training process with the sour cherry. Remove the pendulous laterals and force the upright branches to form the scaffold. After a few years the heading back should be discontinued, because it stimulates new growth which delays fruiting. Cherries are slow to bear, and pruning will never hasten the process.

Citrus Fruits

Oranges, lemons, and other citrus fruits are greatly prized as ornamental or fruiting trees. Unfortunately, they are limited to the Pacific Coast and the southern fringe of the United States; and they find their greatest use in southern California and Florida. Breeding and selection of new varieties is constantly pushing the frontier northward, but it is doubtful if a truly hardy citrus fruit will ever be produced. The use of these trees purely as decorative material is practical in many fringe areas where the fruit would be useless for food. Pruning then follows the usual pattern for broadleaved evergreen trees and shrubs, consisting of corrective shaping and the removal of dead, diseased, or overcrowded branches.

In localities where citrus are grown commercially and the garden tree may be expected to produce fruit of good quality, the training and pruning should follow the example set by the experienced orchardist.

The citrus are all evergreen and bear their fruit near the tips of new growth.

Citrus—Orange

The orange tree heads up naturally and carries its foliage down to the ground. It produces regularly without aid from the pruning shears and it requires no wood renewal. For this reason, many trees are not pruned at all, and most commercial groves are pruned as little as possible. This is a safe practice, providing a few simple steps are taken in the first four or five years.

The tree from the nursery should be headed back to about 3 feet, but all the laterals should be allowed to remain. These may be lightly headed, just enough to even up the tree.

During the next three years, the main task is to keep the laterals growing in an upright direction. If they are not lightened occasionally, the weight of the evergreen leaves will cause them to droop, and in later years the fruit will drag them down. Light heading and thinning will develop a strong framework capable of bearing the heavy weight of a normal crop. Suckers, or any strong and spiny branches that start, should be removed at once. They can easily be detected because of their rank and wild look, and if unchecked they can upset the whole balance of the tree.

After the third year, the bottom branches should be removed, a few at a time, until a clean trunk 2 feet from the ground is obtained. These branches have performed a real service by protecting the trunk from sunburn and cold, but by now the upper branches are able to perform this service. The lower branches will soon arch to ground level again, which is an attractive and beneficial habit.

From the fifth year on, remove spindly growths and any wood in the interior of the tree which has been shaded out. Dead wood is extremely difficult to remove from the center, but the experts feel that it should not be left. Do not make openings in the canopy of leaves, but thin out enough to prevent dense masses of foliage. If a tree should be frosted and some die-back is apparent, do not be in too big a hurry to remove the dead tips. Wait until the new leaf buds start to unfold, and then remove at least one healthy bud with each dead section.

Citrus—Lemon

Lemons, unlike oranges, require considerable pruning to keep them within reasonable bounds. They have a tendency to run wild and carry fruit at the tips of long, straggly branches that are unable to carry the weight.

The young tree should be headed low and the laterals should be cut back sharply. All new growth should be pinched back several times during the growing season to produce a heavy framework. Remove all suckers and heavy sprouts and strive for a compact, twiggy type of growth. Establish a height, which may be about 10 feet, and remove all growth that goes above this height. This is best done twice a year: just as growth is starting in the spring and again in midsummer.

Thin and remove dead wood as needed.

The very popular Meyer lemon, or Chinese dwarf lemon, is one of the hardiest citrus grown and will stand considerable frost. It may be grown as a dwarf tree, a bushy specimen shrub, or a hedge. The habit is dwarf and compact and pruning is simple and corrective only.

Citrus—Grapefruit

Training and pruning as for the orange.

Citrus—Others

There are many other citrus plants that grow in localities that have only a few degrees of frost. Prune as for the orange, except for the dwarf varieties for which no pruning other than shaping is necessary.

This includes the lime, limequat, kumquat, tangerine, tangelo, and calamondin.

Fig

There are several distinct types of fig that require different treatment even in the training stage. The common Mission or California Black and the Adriatic grow like a large shrub with many low spreading branches. The tree should be cut back at planting; and a selection of scaffold branches should be made at the first dormant pruning, as in the case of the other varieties of fruit which we have discussed. These primary branches, however, should not be headed back. Figs bear all of their fruit on the new wood which is generally amply produced without pruning. Low branches which interfere with culture and picking should be removed each year. Top pruning will only be necessary if branches cross or die back from any cause.

The Calimyrna fig is not inclined to produce laterals unless forced to do so. Heavy pruning during the training period may be necessary to establish a framework close enough to the trunk to make a well-balanced tree. Little pruning is necessary after the tree is bearing, unless the growth becomes too rank, in which case a heading back and thinning out of the new wood is indicated.

Because of the tenderness of the fruits and the care with which they must be picked, the vigorous types such as the Kadota are often headed low and pruned for a low-spreading, flat-topped tree. This is standard practice with commercial growers. The flat top is obtained by heading the new growth at different lengths, short in the center of the tree and progressively longer as the outside of the plant is reached. New growth is annually headed back to a foot or a foot and a half in length after this flat top is established.

The Capri figs are treated in a similar manner; but as the growth is more restrained, it is not necessary to remove so much wood. Some control of late crops is possible by pruning, but is a matter for the commercial grower and cannot be gone into at this time.

Tip-pruning after the first crop has been picked will hasten the formation of new laterals and increase the later crops. This works well with the Brown Turkey and some others.

Flowering Fruit Trees

See Chapter Seven, pages 52 and 53.

Nectarine

There is no essential difference between the nectarine and the peach and the pruning is identical. (See below.)

Olive

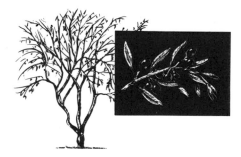

The olive is frequently grown as a decorative shade tree and little attention is paid to whether it sets fruit or not. An unpruned tree generally produces only in alternate years and the fruits are small and of poor quality. The fruit is all borne on the new shoots of the previous year. Annual pruning to encourage growth will result in a yearly harvest of good quality.

Although this is an evergreen, the pruning is generally done in winter. The central-leader or modified-leader system is used, and a single trunk is to be preferred, although there is a strong tendency to break near the ground and to produce vigorous sucker growths. Training should follow the regular pattern for the first few years, but the pruning should be extremely light. When the tree begins to bear, it will only be necessary to thin out one-third to one-half of the small branches that have produced fruit. This renews the fruiting wood and permits light and air to reach the center of the tree. All of the short growths on the lower framework branches should be removed to keep the center of the tree open. Remove all suckers as soon as discovered.

Peach

We include nectarine with the peach as the fruiting habit and consequent pruning requirements are exactly the same. No other crop is more dependent on pruning than the peach. The fruit is borne on the previous year's growth and new fruiting wood must be produced each year. Some varieties tend to set more fruit basally, others terminally. Heavy pruning is the rule to prevent the bearing area from becoming too high in the tree. An open center must be maintained so that bearing wood will not be shaded out by the dense foliage.

The training should follow the open-center system, and not more than three main branches should be allowed to form the scaffold. Once these branches have been selected and allowed to become equally dominant, very little pruning should be done until the tree comes into bearing, usually the third year. The winter following the first crop, the center of the tree should be well opened up, if neglected during training, to allow the penetration of light and air. As the tree ages, inside growths may need to be encouraged. In hot climates, however, this should not be severe enough to expose the branches to sunburn.

Peaches, under conditions to their liking, have a tendency to over-bear, and heavy pruning is essential to prevent the setting of more fruit than the tree can mature properly. This reduces the amount of hand thinning that will be necessary as the fruit develops.

The amateur rarely thins the peach enough, either the branches in winter, or the fruit in summer. The result is an inferior product.

The bearing tree should have all the spindly shoots removed. The remaining branched shoots should be headed back to a sturdy lateral or to a sound outward-pointing bud. If the laterals are numerous on the headed branch, they should be thinned out. The remaining fruit-bearing shoots can be headed slightly if the variety is in-

clined to over-bear. A few varieties tend to bear near the outer end of the bearing shoots, so observation is necessary before heading these varieties.

Pear

The pear is trained to a modified-leader system, with the center left as open as possible. Although the bearing habit is similar to the apple, many more scaffolds may be left on the pear. Twenty or more are not uncommon, which would be gross overcrowding in most other species. Most lateral growth is spur growth and it rarely causes enough shading to prevent fruit set. The fruit is borne on spurs carried by wood that is two or more years old. These spurs are productive for many years and thus do not need frequent renewal as in the case of the peach and apricot.

Most varieties are nearly fastigiate in habit, and care must be exercised to see that the leader remains strongly dominant so that it will not be choked out by the narrow-angled lower branches. The crotches should be as wide-angled as possible, especially for the Bartlett. New growths are made mainly from the terminal buds, and though severe heading back is not advisable, it is sometimes necessary to force branching by this method. Always head back to an outside bud or lateral to open up the tight crown of the tree.

The mature tree needs but little pruning other than a light thinning and corrective pruning. The more vigorous the growth of the tree, the less it should be pruned, because the rank new growth thus stimulated is susceptible to pear blight.

Pecan

Pecans are pruned similarly to walnuts, but naturally assume a true pyramidal character. (See below.)

Persimmon

When trained by the modified-leader system, only the renewal of bearing wood is required. The fruit is carried on the current growth, which must be produced in quantity each year. The tree will tend to bear on the outside unless the thinning is sufficient to admit enough light to produce fruiting shoots in the center.

Always cut to laterals and do not leave stubs. If too much heading is resorted to, the tree will produce a mass of shoots and watersprouts and it will fail to set fruit.

Persimmons have a tendency to self-thin the partly matured fruit, due probably to weather or soil conditions. Sometimes all of the fruit will drop if conditions are unfavorable. It has been found, in some areas, that a bark strangulation seems to cause this difficulty. Slashing the bark in a few places seems to relieve this condition. Use a sharp knife and cut through the bark in several places up and down the trunk and main branches. These slashes can be 6 or 8 inches long and should run lengthwise.

Plum

Plum is a group name covering the complex group of species and hybrids that form the prunus family. It would be impossible, in a book of this brevity, to go thoroughly into the individual habits and requirements of the many varieties. We will treat them in two groups: the Japanese and the European.

The prune is included under the European group because its fruiting habit is the same. A prune is merely a plum that has a sufficiently high sugar content to dry out without fermentation around the pit. Furthermore, prunes are not picked from the tree as are plums. They are allowed to ripen on the tree and to drop or be shaken to the ground. For this reason the trees are usually allowed to grow much larger than are trees whose fruits must be picked.

Japanese Plums

This group includes most of the well-known table plums found in the home garden. The Burbank, Wick-son, Santa Rosa, Abundance, Kelsey, Satsuma, and Climax are all classified under this heading. They vary widely in habit of growth, and some of them have such a decided spreading habit that it is necessary continually to force the growth upward. Others grow narrowly upward and require spreading as suggested for the pear.

The fruit of this group is borne on stubby spurs that rarely exceed 3 inches in length. The spurs have a bearing life of from 6 to 8 years. Some fruit may develop at the base of the year-old shoots.

Strangely enough, we deviate from the average procedure when pruning plums. They must be pruned heavily to insure good-sized fruit, even though the life span of the spur would seem to indicate that only a sixth or eighth of the wood should be renewed. Many varieties make a tremendous amount of growth each year which must be controlled by severe thinning. The pruning recommended for the apricot is about right for this group, although the spurs last two or three times as long.

European Plums

The plums of this group (which contains the well-known prunes) vary from the rest mainly in the length of the fruiting spur. In some varieties these spurs extend and branch into so-called "fruiting brush" which, in their life span, may reach more than 3 feet. This brush does not need the severe thinning given to the Japanese varieties in the home orchard, because the spread of the fruit buds prevents the overcrowding that would occur on the short spurs.

Because they grow so large, the true prune trees are sometimes neglected for several years and then heavily pruned. This usually causes a lush new growth and a sharply reduced yield for two or three seasons. It is far better annually to thin out the older spurs and smaller branches, and to keep the center open enough to be able to set fruit in the central portions of the tree. As prune trees sunburn badly, the bark should not be unduly exposed in hot climates.

Quince

The quince has a very peculiar fruiting habit like no other common fruit. A short growth develops from the terminal and lateral buds which flower at its tip. Thus the fruits are produced only on the current soft, leafy branches which develop on one-year wood. They have no stem and form tight to the leaves. The new growth shoots develop from lateral buds on the previous year's growth. This gives the characteristic zig-zag look to the plant.

Quinces need careful training to become trees, as they tend to be dwarfed and bushy in habit. The top should be kept open and the tree should be thinned.

After the tree begins to bear, it requires only enough thinning out and heading back to laterals to stimulate new growth. Remember that the quince bears at the tips of the new growth; so obviously if the tree is sharply headed, no fruit will be produced. It is also highly susceptible to fire blight and over-stimulation is to be avoided.

Walnut

Walnut trees are frequently found in home gardens in purely decorative plantings or as street trees. The walnut is one of the few food-producing trees that can be permitted to attain a large size in a natural manner. Many commercial growers do very little pruning. Low branches and dead or crossing branches are, of course, removed. Maximum crops are to be obtained only when the tops are thinned enough to allow some light into the center of the trees, especially in the coastal areas.

Training: The training of the young tree from the nursery is a bit different from the average fruit tree and is sometimes perplexing to the amateur. When purchased,

the tree's main stem is usually 7 or 8 feet tall and thick and healthy looking. Nevertheless, it should be cut back to a couple of buds or not over 18 inches. The most vigorous new shoot should be selected during the first summer and the rest should be trimmed back. This shoot is soft and brittle and should be securely staked. It will normally grow several feet and need not be headed.

The following spring the laterals will begin to form and the framework branches can be selected. The lowest branch should be at least 5 feet from the ground, and 6 feet would be better. Allow about 2 feet between branches, because the mature branches are likely to droop too low and become overcrowded if too close together.

As the bark of the walnut and the shell of the nut sunburn easily, they need protection from over exposure in the hotter areas. During the training period, it is advisable to leave all the shoots on the main stem. Pinch out the tips of the ones not wanted for branches, and remove them after the framework has developed enough to shade the trunk. An alternative would be to whitewash the trunk to prevent sunburn after removing the unwanted branchlets.

Pruning: During the second dormant pruning, all side growths should be pruned from the main branches. Laterals should always be a year younger than the branch from which they come. This should be remembered at each dormant pruning and as each framework branch is selected. The new wood is so soft and pithy that branches of the same age make a very weak crotch.

Name	Habit	Training	Position of Fruit Buds Annual shoots	Spurs	Productive Life of Spur	Pruning
Almond	Upright, spreading	Open center or modified leader	Some	Most	5 years	Light
Apple	Spreading	Modified leader	Some	Most	12-15 years	Very light
Apricot	Upright, spreading, vigorous	Modified leader	Some	Most	3-4 years	Heavy
Avocado	Upright, spreading	Heading	All	———	———	Shaping only
Cherry, Sour	Spreading	Modified leader	Some	Most	10-12 years	Very light
Cherry, Sweet	Upright	Modified leader	Some	Most	10-12 years	Very light
Fig	Low, spreading	Open or delayed open	All	———	———	Various. See text
Nectarine	Upright, spreading	Open center	Most	Some	———	Very heavy
Olive	Spreading	Leader or modified leader	All	———	———	Light thinning
Peach	Upright, spreading	Open center	Most	Some	———	Very heavy
Pear	Various	Modified leader	Some	Most	10-12 years	Very light
Pecan	Upright, spreading	Leader	Young trees	Mature trees	———	Shaping only
Persimmon	Open	Modified leader	All	———	———	Light thinning
Plum, European	Various	Modified leader	Some	Most	6-8 years	Light thinning
Plum, Japanese	Various	Open or delayed open	Some	Most	6-8 years	Heavy thinning
Quince	Shrubby	Open or delayed open	All	———	———	Light thinning
Walnut	Upright, spreading	Leader	Young trees	Mature trees	———	Light thinning

CHAPTER 9. Berries and Grapes

Edible berries are widely grown in suburban areas and on farms throughout the country. They occupy a limited space, if correctly trained and pruned, and their culture is thus practical in restricted quarters.

With few exceptions the plants are unattractive from an ornamental standpoint, and even proper care will not make them acceptable to many gardeners. Too often, they are relegated to waste spaces and out-of-the-way corners where considerable or complete neglect is their lot. However, they provide a splendid adjunct to the vegetable garden, and with some care and attention, they can be kept in neat and orderly, if not beautiful, condition.

There are a few points of difference in the fruiting or growth habits, and consequently in the pruning requirements, of the commonly grown varieties, a fact which is frequently overlooked by the amateur gardener.

Blackberry, Boysenberry, Loganberry, and Youngberry

The popularity of the common blackberry has been challenged by the newer hybrids, but it still seems to hold a prominent place in the small fruit garden. These berries are free-growing vines which, if not held severely in check, will rapidly become a hopeless and impenetrable tangle. The nature of these plants makes it possible to control them quite easily and effectively if the pruning is done regularly and at the proper time. These berries should be considered *biennials,* even though the roots are soundly perennial. The shoot that grows from the crown of the plant takes one season to develop, and it sets flowers and fruits the following season. Its work is then completed and it becomes barren or dies outright.

Training: Training depends on the amount of growth that is normal in the area in which the berries are grown. It is possible to train them as unsupported bushes in localities where growth is restrained; and in cold areas where the vines must be laid down and covered, this is a convenient way to grow them. On the Pacific Coast where great quantities of all of these berries are grown, the habit is so vigorous that staking or trellising is essential.

Two types of trellis are in common use, the straight three-wire type and a cross-arm trellis which carries two wires about 18 inches apart. The height for these trellises may be determined by the grower, but the average is between 4 and 5 feet.

Pruning: Pruning consists of the complete removal of all canes that bore fruit immediately after the crop is harvested. There must be 100 per cent renewal each year. The new shoots are thinned to not more than five of the strongest ones, and these are trained into position and headed according to the method of training to be followed:

1. When grown as an unsupported bush, the new canes should be tipped at a height of between 2 and 3 feet. Laterals will start growth immediately; and they should be headed back in early spring, leaving about a foot of the growth which is the bearing wood.

2. When carefully fanned out and tied to a trellis, the new shoots may be allowed to reach 5 or 6 feet before heading. The laterals should be headed the same as above.

3. Some growers using the trellis do not head the selected shoots but drape them over or weave them through the wires of the trellis. The laterals may or may not be headed in this manner, but the vines tend to overbear and the fruit will usually be smaller and more difficult to pick.

The long growing season in California encourages the laterals of some of the newer varieties to develop side shoots, especially if the laterals are pinched or headed early in the season. In this case the fruiting buds will be carried on these secondary shoots which should be headed back and thinned out during the winter or spring pruning.

Himalayan Blackberry

Here is the ever-present exception to the general rule. If pruned like the above varieties, no fruit would be forthcoming. This variety makes a tremendous growth. Some canes have been known to reach 40 feet in one season. Laterals are not formed until the second year and these laterals produce fruit for *several years*. Four canes are enough to leave and they should be securely tied to a permanent trellis and headed when they reach the desired spread. The laterals, which are freely produced, should be headed in turn. All suckers are removed as soon as they appear. After three or four years of bearing, renewal canes should be selected and retained. These canes may be grown along the ground beneath the trellis until needed to replace an old fruiting cane.

Raspberry

The raspberry is widely grown in the northern sections of the country and in cooler areas elsewhere. The vines do not thrive in hot and arid locations. The bearing habit is similar to the blackberry in that the canes are biennial and bear only once. Thus constant renewal is necessary.

The red-fruited varieties do not produce laterals readily, and heading only seems to stimulate growth of suckers rather than laterals. For this reason, it is advisable to head back only the more vigorous shoots and these lightly. Thin out all weak growth.

The black-fruited varieties are not inclined to sucker and will produce laterals when headed. They are usually sharply headed back to 2 or 2½ feet as early as possible during the growing season. The laterals that are then produced are cut back to 5- or 6-inch spurs during the dormant pruning. Many gardeners advise leaving much longer spurs, but the result would be smaller berries.

Both types of raspberries should have all fruiting canes removed as soon after harvesting as possible. This permits a vigorous growth of new shoots for next year's crop.

Raspberries, if desired, can be trained to single stakes or several different trellis systems. The home gardener needs only to provide a support that will keep the vines upright to make picking and cultivating as easy and pleasant as possible.

Currant

Currants are popular in the coldest parts of the country and they are well worth trying in cool areas. Currants make attractive shrubs and can be grown in the garden for ornament, especially where their hardiness is a valuable factor.

They may be trained to a tree form on a single trunk or, preferably, as a many-stemmed shrub. The first year or two, they may be allowed to grow naturally; and the only pruning needed will be for shaping and removal of suckers and excess growth. Currant vines are inclined to make more wood than is desirable; so they should be given a good thinning to six or eight main branches.

The red and white currants bear on spurs produced by wood that is *two* or more years old. The best crops are borne on two- and three-year-old branches. This sets the pattern for pruning. Each winter remove the four-year-old wood and strive for an equal balance of one-, two- and three-year-old branches. Summer pinching of the new shoots will make the plant neat and shapely.

The black currant, *Ribes nigrum*, is rarely grown because of the superior qualities of the red and white forms. It bears on one-year-old wood and needs more severe pruning to insure a good crop of new shoots each year.

Gooseberry

The gooseberry belongs to the same plant family as the currant, so it is not surprising that the pruning is much the same. However, it bears both on the new shoots and on spurs from the older parts of the plant. All wood over three years old should be removed at the dormant pruning. Growth is very profuse and thinning of the new shoots is necessary to insure large berries. If the older branches do not have renewal shoots near their bases, they may be cut back to a stub a few inches long. These stubs will produce many shoots from dormant buds that should be thinned to three or four of the best placed ones.

Blueberries

The development of new hybrid varieties with greatly increased size and quality has stimulated considerable interest in this group—but they are not for everyone. They have a few exacting requirements that must be met for successful culture. They insist on acid soil, good drainage, but ample moisture. More than one variety must be grown, because cross-pollination is essential for the setting of fruit. The plants are hardy anywhere in the United States, and they are beautiful shrubs either as specimen or hedge plants.

In the North, the pruning is simple and consists of light shaping and the removal of weak growth.

In mild climates, pruning is necessary to prevent overbearing and decline of the plant. Fruit is borne on year-old wood; so constant renewal of the wood is desirable. A few of the older canes should be removed each winter. Maximum size in the fruit is obtained by cutting away one-half of each flower cluster while in bloom, and by cutting the bearing shoot back to three or four clusters.

Grapes

The pruning of grapes commercially has become a very exact science. In some localities, the weight of the prun-

Shown here is a long fruiting cane that is part of permanent framework of an arbor grape. Shoot (A), which developed on cane during previous season, being shortened back to two buds, which will produce fruit next summer

ings determines the number of buds to be left on the plant. This degree of exactitude may not interest the owner of a few vines but it gives us a valuable guide. Grapes must be pruned and pruned hard to produce maximum yields.

All grapes bear their fruit at the base of the new shoots which develop from winter buds on the year-old canes. All varieties will overbear to the detriment of the fruit unless drastically curtailed.

There are two popular ways of growing grapes: in bush form or trained on a trellis or arbor. In commercial vineyards, the bush training is predominant; but in the home garden, the trellis method is more widely preferred.

The modern tendency is to train all types of grapes by the cane system in home gardens. A slight loss in production may be expected, but they will produce when grown in this manner. The pruning should be a bit more severe in the European varieties and under no circumstances be omitted.

The American grapes are vigorous climbers and can support more fruiting wood than the European varieties. All varieties should be trained on something substan-

tial, such as a trellis or arbor. Fairly heavy posts carrying two strands of wire, one 3 feet and the other 5 feet from the ground, can be used to train the vine. Here is the procedure:

1. Cut back to two buds or nodes at planting time. Allow all growth to develop.

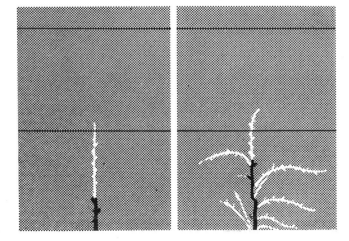

2. At the first pruning, remove all suckers and canes except the strongest *one*. Head it back to two buds. During the following growing season, select the strongest shoot growing from the year-old spur and tie it to an upright on the trellis. Let it make all the

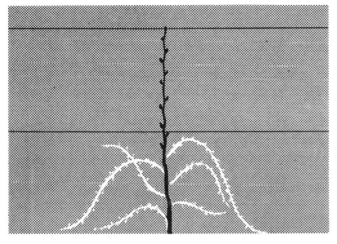

laterals it wants to, but remove any blossom clusters that might form. All outer growth must be removed periodically while in a very young stage.

3. The second pruning consists of heading the main cane or trunk just above the top wire and selecting four laterals, two for each wire. The number

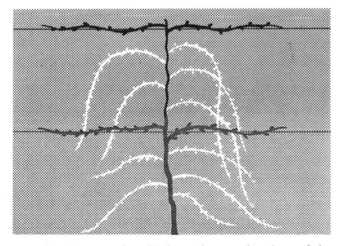

of buds to retain will depend upon the vigor of the vine. Normally the top canes can carry eight or ten buds each and fruit may be allowed to set on them. The lower canes should be cut to two or three bud spurs the first time.

4. From this point on, the amount to prune will depend upon the amount of annual growth produced and the quality of the crop. If the growth is rank and the grapes are poor, leave more buds. If the growth is sparse and the bunches are numerous but ripen badly, cut back more severely.

Weight Method: If you wish to experiment with the weight formula, bear in mind that the method was devised for eastern grape growers and cannot be applied indiscriminately to all varieties under other conditions. However, it has theoretical merit, as it is based on plant growth, and takes into account weak-growing versus strong-growing vines. The following will apply to the Concord, and if the method is used the grower should be ready to modify it as much as is necessary to bring the fruiting habit of his vines into line with expectations. Dealing with bearing vines four years or older, we proceed as follows:

Weigh all the one-year growth and use the "30-plus-10 plan." Leave 30 buds for the first pound and 10 more for each pound thereafter. Thus 2½ pounds of year-old trimmings would indicate that you may retain 45 buds distributed among the 4 laterals. It is only necessary to weigh a sample to be able to judge the approximate yield of wood from the others and to prune accordingly. Always leave a two-bud spur at the base of each cane for renewal. Each year the old bearing cane is cut away and is replaced by a one-year-old cane from this spur. Otherwise the fruit will be carried farther and farther away from the trunk and from the source of plant food.

When trained over an arbor the same procedure should be followed. The vine can be extremely decorative and at the same time produce a bountiful crop of delicious fruit. The vine that is allowed to ramble unchecked will never produce anything like the quality fruit that can be obtained by systematic pruning.

Old neglected vines can generally be brought back to bearing in a short time if severely thinned out and headed back using the same formula as before. Remember, you only weigh (or estimate) the last year's growth, not the two-year or older canes.

A form of pruning that is well worth the trouble is the thinning of the individual cluster of grapes. The quality is greatly improved without loss of total weight if a third or half of the grapes are thinned out before they are more than one-third mature size.

CHAPTER 10. Ornamental Vines

The pruning of vines is a puzzling problem to many gardeners; consequently, vines suffer more neglect in pruning than do most other groups of ornamental plants.

Vines that receive no pruning or thinning soon become so matted, heavy, and choked with dead wood that their generous efforts at flowering are unable to overcome the untidiness of the plant as a whole. The "remedy" is too frequently a hard heading back. This not only loses an entire crop of flowers (in some varieties), but results in an uncontrollable mass of rank new growth that will soon be worse than ever.

Old neglected vines, or those that have been blown or pulled from their supports, must be severely handled. They should be cut back nearly to the crown so as to remove all of the weak, matted, and dead wood. Then a vigilant training program must be followed. Thin down the mass of new shoots to just enough of the strongest ones to fill the allotted space. Train these shoots, tie them in place, and tip them when they have grown a sufficient length. Should the roots be extremely vigorous and the new growth impossible to control, it may be necessary to root-prune. This can be done by spading around the plant to cut the surface feeders or by digging a foot-and-a-half deep trench a few feet from the plant.

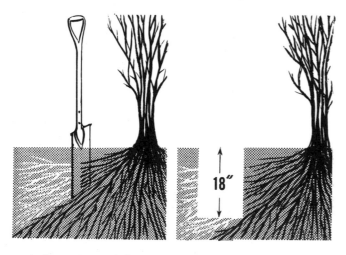

A far more satisfactory result is obtained when the vine is kept under control from the day it is planted in the garden. If all of the stems required are trained into place as individuals and not allowed to cross and tangle, the removal of old shoots and the training of renewals will be an easier and less complicated task. It will also eliminate the temptation to head back severely, with its resulting problems.

Vines are of many diverse types and habits. The listing that follows deals separately with some and groups others that can be pruned in a similar manner. Many other fine vines could be added if space would permit, but the following list should provide enough information to indicate the proper treatment of similar species.

Akebia   *Five-leaf*

This semi-deciduous shrubby climber needs little pruning because of a restrained habit of growth and a comparatively sparse foliage. New shoots that are not needed should be removed, and the tips of the others should be pinched out when long enough to suit your purposes. Only the new shoots can be trained, because the older stems become stiff and woody. After a few years some of the old growth should be removed each season after flowering.

Bignonia   *Trumpet-flower*

The trumpet-flower family has been divided by botanists into several separate genera. For our purposes they can all be grouped together, and, as far as pruning is concerned, treated similarly. The well-known names are as follows:

Campsis   *Orange-red trumpet-vine*

Clytostoma   *Violet trumpet-vine*

Doxantha   *Cats-claw*

Pandorea

Phaedranthus

Tecomaria   *Cape-honeysuckle*

These vines are strong-growing, woody climbers; most of them are evergreen. A severe frost will defoliate and burn the tips of most of them, but they recover rapidly unless their roots have been killed. Control them from the beginning, because once they get out of hand, they are difficult to untangle. Thin out old and weak shoots and prevent suckers from becoming too numerous. All frosted tips can be cut back to firm wood as soon as danger of cold weather is past. New growth can be pinched any time during the growing season to control the size of the vine. Vines bloom on the new wood, so any serious pruning should be done after flowering.

Bomarea

The twining growth of this vine is soft and succulent; and, though it remains evergreen in frost-free areas, it usually dies back to the ground elsewhere. It should be cut to the ground in late fall and its new shoots trained up the following spring. *Never* tip or head the new growth. It will not produce laterals and the flowers are borne in a terminal umbel.

Bougainvillea

This woody vine is normally evergreen, but frost will sometimes defoliate it. The roots can stand considerable frost and will usually sprout freely. Top branches thought to be dead should not be pruned out until growth is well started. In cool climates it is seldom necessary to prune heavily; but thinning and removal of surplus suckers is routine in well-established plants. They may be headed at any desired height, in fact they will stand any amount of pruning. Severe cutting will promote active vegetative growth at the expense of flowers in the cooler and northern limits of its range.

In frost-free areas the pruning is quite different and much more severe. The vines grow with a tropical vigor that must be controlled. An established plant can be given two prunings a year with no resultant loss of bloom. In early spring the vine is heavily thinned and headed, removing all weak growth and cutting back the laterals to the basal buds on the main canes. The response is a mass of tall, straight, flowering shoots which bloom in early summer. As soon as these have finished blooming, their spent stems should be removed. Thorny suckers are freely produced which should be removed while small if not needed. Those needed should be tipped when a few feet high, although they will flower if allowed to develop.

Celastrus   *Bitter-sweet*

The bitter-sweet is a deciduous, shrubby climber grown for the showy berries that are at their best after the leaves have dropped. The free use of these berries usually provides enough pruning. Wood should be thinned to prevent too massive a growth, and heading will control the size of the plant without loss of fruit, as it is borne on short axillary shoots along the stem. Suckers are freely produced and should be removed. It should not be trained through other plants as it is a strangler of no mean ability.

Cissus   *Evergreen grape*

If well trained this vine will need no formal pruning, although frequent light heading is generally necessary for control. It is better to remove a little at frequent intervals rather than prune severely at one time. Severely cut branches are inclined to die back.

Clematis

This family is divided into several groups having widely divergent habits of growth and flowering. Consequently our pruning technique must vary accordingly. Much dissatisfaction with these lovely plants can be traced to improper pruning methods.

Clematis Jackmanii. This well-known clematis is the type plant of a group of large-flowered hybrids derived from crosses of the species *C. lanuginosa* and *C. viticella*. These are all summer-flowering varieties and produce their bloom on new wood developed the same season. The vine may be trained as a low, pillar type or trained high as a true vine. In either case the production of new wood is of primary importance, and all of last year's growth should be cut back to the first joint, during the dormant period.

The rest of the large-flowered varieties are spring-flowering species, *C. patens* and *C. florida* and their many hybrids. They bloom from *year-old wood,* and if pruned like the above group would produce no flowers that season. This group should be lightly thinned and pruned immediately after flowering so that new wood will have time to mature for next season's bloom. A good control is obtained if half of the old wood is pruned back hard each year to provide renewals.

Clematis Armandii is the evergreen species that produces a show of small white flowers in spring. Train carefully during the early years and very little pruning will be required. The vigor of this vine in favorable locations sometimes causes it to overgrow its allotted space. It may then be pruned severely after the blooming season. If necessary to do this in fall or early spring, the loss of one season's flowers would result.

Other small-flowering species, such as *C. alpina* and *C. montana,* flower on ripened wood which must not be pruned away. Thinning during the dormant period is usually all that is required.

The bush varieties are herbaceous in habit and are cut to the ground each fall.

Dolichos   *Australian pea*

This evergreen twining perennial vine is rapid and lush in growth. Control pruning is about all that is possible. When it becomes too heavy or is frost damaged, cut it to the ground in spring and train the new growth.

Gelsemium   *Carolina jessamine*

This is an evergreen twining vine that blooms in winter and early spring. Thinning and training should immediately follow the blooming season. Will stand severe pruning where desired.

Hardenbergia

This shrubby half-climber becomes thin and leggy without corrective pruning. After blooming, the spent flower stems and weak shoots should be removed. During the growing season, a little tip pinching will make the plant more compact and attractive.

Hedera   *English ivy*

The "cemetery variety" is rapidly giving way before the many fine new varieties that have recently come on the market. They may be pruned or sheared as lightly or as heavily as desired at any time. It is strongly advised that they should not be allowed to climb the trunks of shrubs and trees. Ivy growing on a wall should be pruned twice a year by removing all free-hanging branches. This will prevent a thick mattress of woody shoots from forming and will reduce the weight pulling away from the wall.

Ipomea   *Morning-glory*

Though a true perennial, this vine is frequently grown as an annual. Cut back to the ground each fall and train the new growth in spring.

Jasminum   *Jasmine, jessamine*

These shrubby or woody vines are mostly evergreen and require very little pruning beyond thinning out and tidying up the plant. This should be done after blooming. Do not prune severely, because the flowers are produced on old wood, and severe pruning may prevent development of the following year's show of blooms. It is best to prune a third or fourth of the plant each year so that enough old wood will be left to give a good display. The shrubby types should have some of the oldest wood removed.

Lathyrus   *Sweet-pea*

Cut back in the fall as soon as leaves become ragged.

Lonicera   *Honeysuckle*

The vine types lose their leaves in cold climates but are nearly evergreen in frost-free areas. After flowering, they should be headed and thinned severely. Suckers should be removed and stems should not be permitted to reach the ground and root. Rule these vines with an iron hand and sharp shears, and you will be rewarded with a neat plant and superior flowers never seen on a neglected plant.

Mandevilla   *Chilean-jasmine*

A summer-flowering, deciduous vine that can be thinned and trained during the dormant season. Inclined to be leggy, and many growers cut it back to the ground each fall.

Parthenocissus   *Boston ivy, Virginia creeper*

These vines will stand any amount of pruning, and all loose or out-of-place tendrils should be removed during the growing season. If damaged in any way or torn from its support, the only satisfactory treatment is to cut back to the ground and start over. The mature branches cannot attach themselves again if pulled loose. Die-back from drought or other reasons can sometimes be carefully removed without disturbing the healthy portion of the vine.

Passiflora (Tacsonia)   *Passion-vine, Passion-flower*

These evergreen, vigorous vines are very difficult to thin out properly. Usually, they may be left for several years before it becomes necessary to reduce the accumulation of wood. Then the only solution is to remove the entire vine back to ground level or to short spurs of sound young wood. This should be done in the spring after danger of frost is over, and the new growth will quickly cover the original areas.

Plumbago   *Leadwort*

The vine may be trained as a shrub or a climber. When wanted as a climber, the young plant should be thinned to a few of the strongest shoots and these should be tied into position. All suckers should be removed and weak and spent shoots should be removed after flowering.

When grown as a shrub, all new growth can be allowed to develop, and the shoots that grow too vigorously should be tipped at the desired height while still soft. After a few years an annual removal of a few of the oldest canes will allow for wood renewal. These old canes should be removed at ground level after blooming. When badly frosted, the entire plant can be cut back to ground level.

Polygonum   *Silver lace-vine*

This strong woody vine becomes completely deciduous and sometimes freezes to the ground in cold areas. Where freezing is suspected, pruning should be delayed until new growth in spring indicates the extent of the injury. In mild climates necessary thinning and control-pruning can be performed during the dormant period. Canes may be lightly headed if necessary, and tip pinching during the summer will aid in control with the least loss of flowers. Some growers cut to the ground immediately after blooming. New shoots will make ample growth for the following season.

Solanum   *Potato-vine, nightshade*

Solanum jasminoides makes a very thick, tangled

growth that is difficult to thin. When thinning becomes necessary, cut back to the ground, and new growth will break from the roots. Spring is the best time in any but the mildest of climates.

The shrubby types should be headed back to strong laterals or buds when required for compactness. Remove thin and weak growth.

Sollya   *Australian Bluebell Creeper*

This charming little evergreen is more often grown as a shrub than as a climber. When grown as a shrub, the only pruning needed is to tip the new growth that shows a tendency to climb. If preferred as a climbing plant, it will be necessary to thin out the thick basal growth to a few of the strongest shoots. Any serious pruning should be done after danger of frost is past.

Streptosolen

In spring, tidy up the plant and remove spent shoots and winter damage. If it is inclined to become leggy, head back to force new growth lower down. Will stand heavy pruning, but new wood carries the flowers.

Trachelospermum   *Star-jasmine*

This evergreen, shrubby vine requires practically no pruning. Training is all that is required although it may be trimmed or headed at will without misgiving.

Wistaria

A young wistaria should be allowed to grow without much pruning until it has covered the allotted space or reached the desired size. From that time on, if maximum flowering is desired, all new growth should be cut back to spurs of two buds each. This is done in the fall. Summer tipping of the new growth will also aid the production of flowers. Plants that are of some age and have not bloomed may be forced into bloom by root pruning.

In southern California the practice is to prune most heavily at the end of the spring-blooming season. In many varieties this produces a crop of new shoots which bloom again in summer. These new shoots are headed back in the fall, to control the plant and produce larger flower clusters.

CHAPTER 11. Pruning and Training for Special Purposes

The training of plants for specific purposes requires a greater amount of pruning than is necessary for ordinary garden culture. It also demands a thorough understanding of the basic principles of plant behavior. The plant to be subjected to a rigid training program must be especially suited for the purpose and its normal habit and adaptability well known to the gardener.

Topiary

Topiary is one of the oldest—and certainly one of the least popular—forms of special plant training. Topiary uses a plant as a material with which to form birds, animals, and geometric patterns much as a sculptor would use clay or stone. It was very popular in the formal gardens of ancient Rome, from which it spread through the civilized world, and has been extensively practiced for centuries. There are still many fine examples in older gardens throughout the world, but topiary is rarely practiced today. A closely cropped hedge with some architectural detail is the closest approach to be found in the newer gardens at the present time.

Dwarf Fruit Trees

The recent trend in special training is toward dwarf fruit trees. Although a great amount of work is still to be done with them, more and more varieties are being added to the lists, and nearly all nurseries that handle fruit trees stock some of them.

The dwarf character is the result of grafting on a suitable dwarfing stock and is not dependent on pruning, although many root stocks are not truly dwarfing and have only a semi-dwarfing influence.

Pruning requirements closely follow the procedures outlined for normal-sized trees, except that pruning is often a bit more severe. As we have already learned, consistent heavy pruning has an additional dwarfing influence. A combination of a dwarfing stock, extremely low heading and a relatively severe pruning program, including some summer thinning, produces a plant more in the nature of a large shrub than a fruit tree. These may easily be accommodated in a small area, and maintenance and fruit picking may be done without the use of ladders or special tools.

On a smaller scale, these trees may be pruned in the same manner as the full-sized trees. See Chapter Eight for instructions. Flowering types are discussed in Chapter Seven.

Ornamental Espalier

The training of ornamental shrubs and small trees against fences and walls is a method that is ideally suited to present-day gardens of limited area and modern style. A current trend in landscape design is toward more open functional areas, more fences, wind baffles, and garden structures, and, in many instances, fewer plants. Vines can be used very effectively in such gardens, but there are many shrubs which are suitable for training against flat surfaces with far less care and training than vines require.

In English catalogs many shrubs are listed as "wall shrubs" or "wall plants" that we would rarely think of as suitable for this purpose. Ceanothus, cotoneaster, escallonia, pyracantha, and many other shrubs are trained against fences and walls. Along the West Coast and across our southern states many species may be added to the list. Fuchsia, camellia, fremontia, lantana, magnolia, and, in frost-free areas, poinsettia are effectively used in this manner.

The principal requirements for a good wall shrub are the ability to produce laterals freely even from old wood and to thrive under the severe pruning and training necessary to prevent it from assuming its inherent form and size.

It is highly desirable to start with a young plant and begin the training at once. Older shrubs rarely have suitably placed branches, and the removal of surplus branches would cause large wounds up and down the main stems which would be unsightly for some time. Old plants would have little or no foliage near the center, due to shading while growing in a natural form.

The young plant may be started with one or several leaders depending on the variety and the whim of the gardener. The first few years' staking or tying will be essential with most subjects. Placing cleats against the wall or fence so that the plant can be tied from 4 to 8 inches away from the solid surface will allow for air space and result in a healthier plant, with better foliage placement, and an interesting shadow pattern which adds apparent depth to the planting. Avoid tying with wire in hot climates because burning of the branches will result.

After the selected leader or leaders have been tied to the support, choose the laterals that are growing in such a way that they may be used to develop the pattern decided upon. Should the laterals be poorly spaced or insuf-

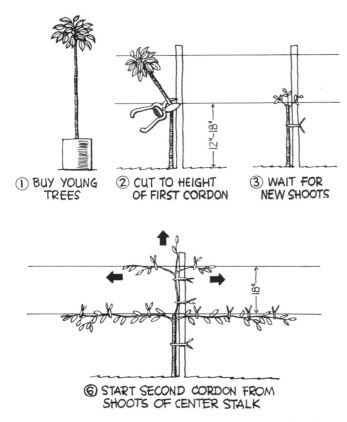

① BUY YOUNG TREES

② CUT TO HEIGHT OF FIRST CORDON

12"–18"

③ WAIT FOR NEW SHOOTS

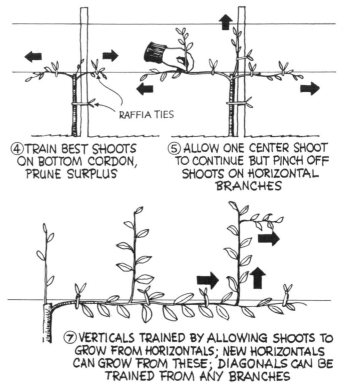

RAFFIA TIES

④ TRAIN BEST SHOOTS ON BOTTOM CORDON, PRUNE SURPLUS

⑤ ALLOW ONE CENTER SHOOT TO CONTINUE BUT PINCH OFF SHOOTS ON HORIZONTAL BRANCHES

18"

⑥ START SECOND CORDON FROM SHOOTS OF CENTER STALK

⑦ VERTICALS TRAINED BY ALLOWING SHOOTS TO GROW FROM HORIZONTALS; NEW HORIZONTALS CAN GROW FROM THESE; DIAGONALS CAN BE TRAINED FROM ANY BRANCHES

ficient in number, it would be best to cut them all back to the main stems to encourage a quantity of new shoots. Allow the shoots that are needed for framework to grow unchecked, but tip out all surplus growth and remove all suckers. As soon as the branches have reached the length desired they may be headed, when they in turn will put out side shoots. For a light effect and a sharply tailored look, all future growth must be headed several times a year. Where a more natural and informal treatment is desirable, the established plant could be left to develop its wood through the year and then be cleaned up and reshaped at the proper pruning season for the variety at hand.

Plants which depend on wood renewal from the base cannot be expected to live as long as if grown in a more natural manner. However, plants such as the magnolia will thrive as an espalier for a hundred years or more.

While more care and pruning are required in the beginning, after a plant has settled into the desired pattern, summer pinching at frequent intervals will usually suffice thereafter.

Oriental Pruning and Modern Adaptation

Although there are comparatively few truly oriental gardens in this country, outside of public parks, there are a great many modern homes that show an oriental influence in their decor. Patios, courts or lanais are frequently graced with plant material so pruned and trained that it adds a subtle oriental touch.

The Japanese are master pruners in their own particular field and every cut has a definite purpose and a deep significance to them. We need not delve deeply into oriental philosophy and religion to recognize the charm and suitability of their distinctive type of plant training. We are not speaking now of *bonsai,* the art of artificially dwarfing forest trees into exquisite miniatures. The present subject deals with plants grown naturally in the ground or in ample containers and given the usual care, but trained to form a low, open habit. The difference lies entirely in the way they are pruned.

Conifers are ideal subjects for the purpose. They look right, they may be selected for any size required, from a one-foot natural dwarf to a three-story pine tree. Many of them endure the amount of shade found in enclosed areas, and they are hardy. The old fear of pruning a conifer, or of cleaning out the inside to expose the branches, is exposed for the absurd superstition it is, in this form of training. The beauty of branch and bark and limb pattern is an important feature unsuspected by those who shear their conifers into perfect domes and avoid like the plague any break in the wall of needles. The reduction of three- or four-fifths of the twigs and needles gives a light and airy appearance which will permit a conifer's use in confined quarters where one of natural growth would be too heavy and somber.

To obtain this result, a conifer of almost any age can

be used, and of any species or variety. Spread the branches so that you can see into the center of the plant and start removing all dead, weak, and crossing branches if these have been allowed to form. Then determine about how open you wish the plant to be and thin the remaining branches until a pleasing pattern is developed. Some gardeners like the branches in flat tiers with considerable space between the tiers. Others prefer a spiral pattern and still others like a pronounced irregularity with masses of comparatively thick growth balanced by open areas. There is a great opportunity for originality but it pays to move carefully. Once you have removed too much there is no remedy because conifers will not break from the old wood.

Attention is given next to the tips of the remaining branches. The weight may cause them to droop but the final pruning will remedy that. Cut back all new growth to a very short spur. Always leave some of this current growth on each spur that is to remain. Now carefully thin out the small branchlets until only a few are left on each branch. Work back and forth over the entire tree so that a fairly uniform result is obtained. Those who prefer a regular, smooth habit should remove side branchlets and leave the straight center one, headed back, of course. The maximum "effect" is obtained by removing the center shoots and letting the side shoots carry on. This gives the irregular zig-zag effect that is highly regarded by many gardeners. The pines are easily controlled, after the pattern is established, by working on the new "candles" (shoots) each spring as described in Chapter Seven.

Late spring, as new growth is beginning to harden, is the best time for major operations in this fascinating phase of gardening. Light pinching throughout the year will make the annual pruning less drastic.

While this type of training tends to dwarf a plant and will permit considerable control over the size to which it will grow, it is strongly advised that the species or variety selected for this training should be one that will fit naturally into the space in which it will be confined. Natural dwarfs are a pleasure to train and control; but the continual battle to prevent a forest giant from overwhelming its site is too frequently lost by the gardener.

Street Trees

Most home gardeners do not have much to say about the selection and care of street trees, as their planting and care have become a function of city government in most communities. The ideal street tree, regardless of type or variety, is one that can grow along normal lines with ample room for full development. This condition is sadly lacking in many cities, and the horribly mutilated trees—cut back to avoid overhead wires or to prevent crowding narrow sidewalks—might better have remained unplanted.

There are some exceptions where trees that normally would easily reach 60 or 70 feet in height have been kept down to 15 to 20 feet for many decades. These trees are distinctive and by many considered beautiful because they have been carefully and intelligently pruned *every* year from the very beginning. The tree that has the ugly, stubby look is usually the one which has been allowed to grow too large and has been severely headed back all at once.

If the homeowner has the care of one or more street trees entrusted to him, he can follow the directions for training and pruning ornamental trees as set forth in Chapter Seven.

R. L. Hudson, Photo

Large pine severely pruned to achieve "oriental" effect. Repeated pruning to side twigs gives zig-zag appearance

Do's and Don'ts

Do's

Use the proper tools for the job at hand and keep them sharp.

Study your plants, especially in regard to time of flowering, type of flowering, and the age of the wood producing flowers.

Prune with confidence, when purpose is clear. An old proverb says, "It is as foolish *not* to prune a peach as it is *to* prune a cherry."

Remove dead, broken, criss-crossing or diseased branches as soon as discovered, regardless of season or blooming habits.

Always paint cuts, larger than 1 inch in diameter, with a good brand of tree wound compound.

Guide, rather than force, in the pruning program. Plants are at their best when allowed to assume their natural or inherent size and form.

Prune hard for new wood and lightly for flowers and fruit.

Prune weak plants hard, and vigorous plants lightly, other conditions being equal.

Don'ts

Do not use hedge shears for general pruning.

Do not do all of your pruning at one time.

Do not prune without a definite reason or for a specific purpose.

Do not expect pruning to make up for cultural mistakes and omissions.

Do not accept casual pruning advice. Check it carefully before putting into practice.

Do not attempt to prune with dull, sprung, or improper tools.

Do not leave stubs when removing large branches and only on small branches when they are meant for spurs.

Do not prune spring-flowering shrubs in fall, winter, or spring, but immediately after flowering, except in special cases that are noted.

Do not assume that every professional "gardener" knows how to prune.

Do not expect a gardener to prune properly in the same amount of time it would take him to slash with hedge shears.

Do not try to make five shrubs grow where there is only room for one. That is expecting too much of pruning.

Do not attempt tree work with makeshift equipment. This is a professional field that requires training, skill, and special tools.

Index

Pruning Terminology: Plant Framework

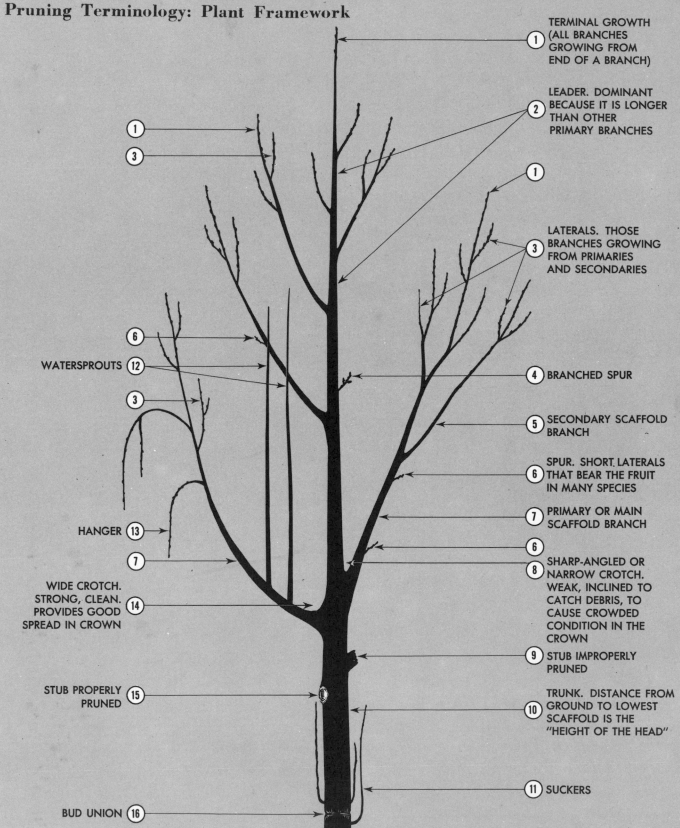

1 TERMINAL GROWTH (ALL BRANCHES GROWING FROM END OF A BRANCH)

2 LEADER. DOMINANT BECAUSE IT IS LONGER THAN OTHER PRIMARY BRANCHES

1

3 LATERALS. THOSE BRANCHES GROWING FROM PRIMARIES AND SECONDARIES

4 BRANCHED SPUR

5 SECONDARY SCAFFOLD BRANCH

6 SPUR. SHORT LATERALS THAT BEAR THE FRUIT IN MANY SPECIES

7 PRIMARY OR MAIN SCAFFOLD BRANCH

6

8 SHARP-ANGLED OR NARROW CROTCH. WEAK, INCLINED TO CATCH DEBRIS, TO CAUSE CROWDED CONDITION IN THE CROWN

9 STUB IMPROPERLY PRUNED

10 TRUNK. DISTANCE FROM GROUND TO LOWEST SCAFFOLD IS THE "HEIGHT OF THE HEAD"

11 SUCKERS

1

3

6

WATERSPROUTS 12

3

HANGER 13

7

WIDE CROTCH. STRONG, CLEAN. PROVIDES GOOD SPREAD IN CROWN 14

STUB PROPERLY PRUNED 15

BUD UNION 16

Dear Mrs. LaRue

Letters from Obedience School

Written and Illustrated by
Mark Teague

Scholastic Press  New York

The Snort City

September 30

For Tracy Mack, Brilliant Editor;
David Saylor, Impeccable Designer; and Earl and Ali, Dogs of Genius

Library of Congress Cataloging-in-Publication Data:
Teague, Mark
Dear Mrs. Larue: letters from obedience school / written and illustrated by Mark Teague.   p. cm.
Summary: Gertrude LaRue receives funny typewritten and paw-written letters from her dog, Ike, entreating her to let him leave the Igor Brotweiler Canine Academy and come back home. • ISBN-13: 978-0-545-01864-7 • ISBN-10: 0-545-01864-1
[1. Dogs—Fiction. 2. Dogs—Training—Fiction. 3. Pets—Fiction. 4. Letters—Fiction. 5. Humorous stories.] I. Title.   PZ7.T2193825 De 2002   [E]—dc21   2001043479

10 9 8 7 6 5 4 3 2 1   07 08 09 10 11/0
Printed in Singapore   46

First printing, April 2007
The display type was set in American Typewriter Bold. The text type was set in 14-point ITC American Typewriter Medium and 18-point Litterbox. The illustrations were painted in acrylics. Book design by Mark Teague and David Saylor

LOCAL DOG ENTERS OBEDIENCE SCHOOL

"Ike"
LaRue

Citing a long list of behavioral problems, Snort City resident Gertrude R. LaRue yesterday enrolled her dog, Ike, in the Igor Brotweiler Canine Academy. Established in 1953, the Academy has a history of dealing with such issues.

"I'm at my wit's end!" said Mrs. LaRue. "I love Ike, but I'm afraid he's quite spoiled. He steals food right off the kitchen counter, chases the neighbor's cats, howls whenever I'm away, and last week while I was crossing the street he pulled me down and tore my best camel's hair coat! I just don't know what else to do!"

School officials were unavailable for comment. . . .

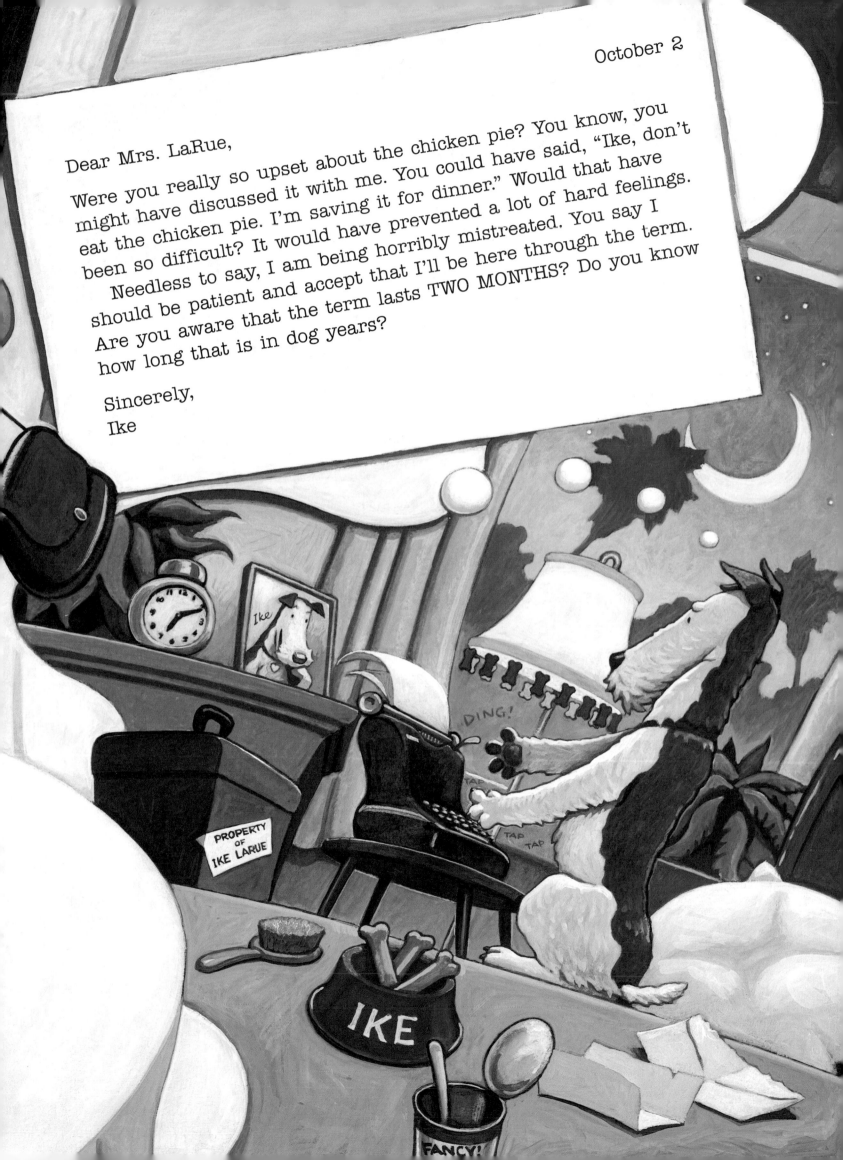

Dear Mrs. LaRue,

Were you really so upset about the chicken pie? You know, you might have discussed it with me. You could have said, "Ike, don't eat the chicken pie. I'm saving it for dinner." Would that have been so difficult? It would have prevented a lot of hard feelings.
   Needless to say, I am being horribly mistreated. You say I should be patient and accept that I'll be here through the term. Are you aware that the term lasts TWO MONTHS? Do you know how long that is in dog years?

Sincerely,
Ike

October 3

Dear Mrs. LaRue,

I'd like to clear up some misconceptions about the Hibbins' cats. First, they are hardly the little angels Mrs. Hibbins makes them out to be. Second, how should I know what they were doing out on the fire escape in the middle of January? They were being a bit melodramatic, don't you think, the way they cried and refused to come down? It's hard to believe they were really sick for three whole days, but you know cats.

Your dog,
Ike

Sit

GRUESOME
PRISON
TALES
卌

October 4

Dear Mrs. LaRue,

You should see what goes on around here. The way my teach — I mean WARDEN, Miss Klondike, barks orders is shocking. Day after day I'm forced to perform the most meaningless tasks. Today it was "sit" and "roll over," all day long. I flatly refused to roll over. It's ridiculous. I won't do it. Of course I was SEVERELY punished.

And another thing: Who will help you cross the street while I'm away? You know you have a bad habit of not looking both ways. Think of all the times I've saved you. Well, there was that one time, anyway. I must say you weren't very grateful, complaining on and on about the tiny rip in your ratty old coat. But the point is, you need me!

Yours,
Ike

October 5

Dear Mrs. LaRue,

The GUARDS here are all caught up in this "good dog, bad dog" thing. I hear it constantly: "Good dog, Ike. Don't be a bad dog, Ike." Is it really so good to sit still like a lummox all day? Nevertheless, I refuse to be broken!

Miss Klondike has taken my typewriter. She claims it disturbs the other dogs. Does anybody care that the other dogs disturb ME?

Yours,
Ike

Dear Mrs. LaRue,

Were the neighbors really complaining about my howling? It is hard to imagine. First, I didn't howl that much. You were away those nights, so you wouldn't know, but trust me, it was quite moderate. Second, let's recall that these are the same neighbors who are constantly waking ME up in the middle of the afternoon with their loud vacuuming. I say we all have to learn to get along.

My life here continues to be a nightmare. You wouldn't believe what goes on in the cafeteria.

Sincerely,
Ike

P.S. I don't want to alarm you, but the thought of escape has crossed my mind!

October 6

50 GREAT ESCAPES

Menu
APPETIZERS:
"FLOOR-DROPPED" TABLE SCRAPS
a Rottweiler Specialty
GOLDEN CHEWY BONE
with gravy
ENTREES:
ROAST

October 7

Dear Mrs. LaRue,

I hate to tell you this, but I am terribly ill. It started in my paw, causing me to limp all day. Later I felt queasy, so that I could barely eat dinner (except for the yummy gravy). Then I began to moan and howl. Finally, I had to be taken to the vet. Dr. Wilfrey claims that he can't find anything wrong with me, but I am certain I have an awful disease. I must come home at once.

Honestly yours,
Ike

October 8

Dear Mrs. LaRue,

Thank you for the lovely get well card. Still, I'm a little surprised that you didn't come get me. I know what Dr. Wilfrey says, but is it really wise to take risks with one's health? I could have a relapse, you know.

With fall here, I think about all the fine times we used to have in the park. Remember how sometimes you would bring along a tennis ball? You would throw it and I would retrieve it EVERY TIME, except for once when it landed in something nasty and I brought you back a stick instead. Ah, how I miss those days.

Yours truly,
Ike

P.S. Imagine how awful it is for me to be stuck inside my tiny cell!
P.P.S. I still feel pretty sick.

October 9

Dear Mrs. LaRue,

By the time you read this I will be gone. I have decided to attempt a daring escape! I'm sorry it has come to this, since I am really a very good dog, but frankly you left me no choice. How sad it is not to be appreciated! From now on I'll wander from town to town without a home — or even any dog food, most likely. Such is the life of a desperate outlaw. I will try to write to you from time to time as I carry on with my life of hardship and danger.

Your lonely fugitive,
Ike

The Snort City Register/Gazette

LARUE ESCAPES DOGGY DETENTION

Former Snort City resident Ike LaRue escaped last night from the dormitory at the Igor Brotweiler Canine Academy. The dog is described as "toothy" by local police. His current whereabouts are unknown.

"To be honest, I thought he was bluffing when he told me he was planning to escape," said a visibly upset Gertrude R. LaRue, the dog's owner. "Ike tends to be a bit melodramatic, you know. Now I can only pray that he'll come back." Asked if she would return Ike to Brotweiler Academy, Mrs. LaRue said that she would have to wait and see. "He's a good dog basically, but he can be difficult. . . ."

TAXI

Ed's TAXI

DOGONE

October 11 — Somewhere in America

Dear Mrs. LaRue,

I continue to suffer horribly as I roam this barren wasteland. Who knows where my wanderings will take me now? Hopefully to someplace with yummy food! Remember the special treats you used to make for me? I miss them. I miss our nice, comfy apartment. But mostly, I miss you!

Your sad dog,
Ike

P.S. I even miss the Hibbins' cats, in a way.

October 12 — Still Somewhere

Dear Mrs. LaRue,

The world is a hard and cruel place for a "stray" dog. You would scarcely believe the misery I've endured. So I have decided to return home. You may try to lock me up again, but that is a risk I must take. And frankly, even more than myself, I worry about you. You may not know it, Mrs. LaRue, but you need a dog!

Your misunderstood friend,
Ike

HERO DOG SAVES OWNER!

Ike LaRue, until recently a student at the Igor Brotweiler Canine Academy, returned to Snort City yesterday in dramatic fashion. In fact he arrived just in time to rescue his owner, Gertrude R. LaRue of Second Avenue, from an oncoming truck. Mrs. LaRue had made the trip downtown to purchase a new camel's hair coat. Apparently she neglected to look both ways before stepping out into traffic.

The daring rescue was witnessed by several onlookers, including patrolman Newton Smitzer. "He rolled right across two lanes of traffic to get at her," said Smitzer. "It was really something. I haven't seen rolling like that since I left the police academy."

Mrs. LaRue was unhurt in the incident, though her coat was badly torn. "I don't care about that," she said. "I'm just happy to have my Ike back home where he belongs!"

LaRue said she plans to throw a big party for the dog. "All the neighbors will be there, and I'm going to serve Ike's favorite dishes. . . ."

I LIKE IKE